Chantal Vaage

Carole Fréchette

two
plays

John and Beatrice
Helen's Necklace

CAROLE FRÉCHETTE: TWO PLAYS

JOHN AND BEATRICE

(JEAN ET BÉATRICE)

HELEN'S NECKLACE

(LE COLLIER D'HÉLÈNE)

Translated by John Murrell

Playwrights Canada Press
Toronto • Canada

Playwrights Canada Press
The Canadian Drama Publisher
215 Spadina Ave., Suite 230, Toronto, Ontario CANADA M5T 2C7
416.703.0013   fax 416.408.3402
orders@playwrightscanada.com • www.playwrightscanada.com

Financial support provided by the taxpayers of Canada and Ontario through the Canada Council for the Arts and the Department of Canadian Heritage through the Book Publishing Industry Development Programme, and the Ontario Arts Council.

Cover painting by Michèle Assal. Panel 1 from *Dimanche prémédité 97*, 122x204cm, www.fly.to/assal. Cover design: JLArt
Production Editor: MZK

Library and Archives Canada Cataloguing in Publication

Fréchette, Carole, 1949-
[Plays. English. Selections]
    Carole Fréchette : two plays / translated by John Murrell.

Translation of: Le collier d'Hélène et Jean et Béatrice.
Contents: Helen's necklace -- John and Beatrice.
ISBN 978-0-88754-501-6

    I. Murrell, John, 1945- II. Title. III. Title: Two plays.

PS8561.R37A253 2007   C842'.54   C2007-900250-1

First edition: January 2007
Printed and bound by AGMV Marquis at Quebec, Canada.

•CONTENTS•

John and Beatrice ································· 1

Helen's Necklace ······························ 59

JOHN AND BEATRICE

John and Beatrice was first produced in English at the Tarragon Theatre Extra Space, Toronto from February 13 to March 24, 2007 with the following company:

BEATRICE   Caroline Cave

JOHN   Rick Roberts

Direction   Leah Cherniak
Set and Costume Design   Yannik Larivée
Lighting Design   Paul Mathiesen
Sound Design   John Gzowski
Video Design   Cylla von Tiedemann
Stage Management   Trina Sookhai

• Characters •

JOHN
BEATRICE

The action takes place in a very large, nearly empty room. Upstage Centre is a vast wrap-around window, only one small pane of which can be opened to let in fresh air.

At one side is the only door, which is locked.
A single, imposing armchair is placed in front of the window. Tacked to the walls are numerous photos, all the same size. On a small table is a Polaroid camera. In one corner is a basket of shiny red apples. On the floor are dozens of water bottles, some empty, some full. Also scattered about are numerous apple cores, quietly moulding in the sun.

It is a beautiful day. Outside the window, skyscrapers gleam in the light of late afternoon. From time to time, birds may fly past the thirty-third floor, where the room is situated.

In the armchair, staring out the window, is a young woman, avidly eating an apple. This is BEATRICE. The sound of her crunching, echoes in the nearly empty room.

BEATRICE has long hair which descends in gentle waves to her waist, like the hair of a Medieval princess.

After a while, someone knocks on the locked door.

BEATRICE   Yes?

There is no answer. Someone knocks again.

Who's there?

No answer. BEATRICE stands and walks slowly to the door, still crunching her apple. She takes out a key which she has hidden over her heart, turns it in the lock, and opens the door. Outside the door is a man, bent over, struggling for breath. This is JOHN. He's carrying a black suitcase.

BEATRICE gestures for him to enter, closes the door and locks it, then hides the key over her heart. JOHN

> *remains bent over; a cramp in his right side is*
> *causing him severe pain. He tries to speak, but*
> *BEATRICE pre-empts him.*

I know, the elevator's out of order, so you had to do all thirty-three flights on foot, and you didn't see another soul on the stairs. At first, you thought the building must be abandoned, and maybe this whole thing was just a bad joke, or even a trap. Somewhere around the eighteenth floor, a vague sense of dread came over you, and for a while you considered just getting the hell out of here. But then you got your second wind. You took the last fifteen flights two steps at a time, like the natural athlete you are. What exhausted you was not really the climb but the heat, which is almost unbearable in the staircase. Now you're thoroughly dehydrated, speaking of which, do I have a glass of water handy?

> *She extends a bottle of water, which JOHN refuses.*

Sorry. I'm talking too much. *(She takes a big gulp of water.)*

JOHN   How much?

BEATRICE   Sorry?

JOHN   How much is "substantial"?

BEATRICE   What are you talking about?

> *JOHN takes a large piece of paper out of his pocket.*

JOHN   Is this your poster?

BEATRICE   Yes.

JOHN   It says right here, in black and white, "Substantial Reward Offered."

BEATRICE   That's what it says.

JOHN   So – how much?

BEATRICE   Slow down.

JOHN   Sorry?

BEATRICE   We'll get to that later.

She picks up the Polaroid camera.

JOHN   Later?

BEATRICE   Smile!

She takes his picture. He doesn't smile.

Don't worry. It's for my archives.

JOHN   How much is a "substantial reward"?

BEATRICE   *(looking at the photo she took)* Do you frown in all your photos?

JOHN   *(reading the poster)* "Notice to all men in the city: Well-to-do young heiress, intelligent and perceptive, who has never lived—"

BEATRICE   "Loved."

JOHN   Sorry?

BEATRICE   "Who has never loved anyone."

JOHN   *(continuing to read)* "—who has never loved anyone, neither her mother, nor her father, nor her cat—"

BEATRICE   *(reciting from memory)* "—nor her aunt from the States, who sends her a hundred dollar bill every Christmas, nor her maid Janine who bakes chocolate-chip cookies for her, nor the fourteen different lovers she has had during fourteen years of sexual activity—"

JOHN   *(continuing to read)* "—is seeking a man who will interest, move, and seduce her. In that order. Substantial Reward Offered." *(showing the poster to BEATRICE)* "SUBSTANTIAL REWARD"—all caps.

BEATRICE   *(not looking at it)* Exactly. And, underneath, in smaller print, "All interested parties apply to the thirty-third floor," etc.

JOHN   Exactly. So, how much is a "substantial reward"?

BEATRICE   *(moving to the window)* Come here.

JOHN moves to her.

Look down there.

He looks.

That's mine.

JOHN   What is?

BEATRICE   The street down there, that's mine.

JOHN   What do you mean, yours?

BEATRICE   Everything down there, from the souvlaki place to the end of the block, plus the gay bar on the next corner, it's all mine.

JOHN   You mean, the buildings?

BEATRICE   All the buildings. Including this one.

JOHN   Retail outlets, studios, condos – all yours?

BEATRICE   Everything. My father left it to me. In black and white, in his will, "I leave all the streets of which I am proprietor to my daughter Beatrice."

JOHN   Your dad?

BEATRICE   John Dutrisac. The plastic garbage can king.

JOHN   Never heard of him.

BEATRICE   Do you have a plastic garbage can?

JOHN   What?

BEATRICE   Of course you have a plastic garbage can. Everybody has one. Some people live in them. Garbage cans made my father's fortune. Everything you ever tossed out, all your debris, your old ball-points, letters you never finished, your mouldy spaghetti, my father took it all in. Wasn't he brilliant to think of that? A way to contain all the garbage of the western world in plastic. With the money from his garbage cans, he bought up whole streets. He fantasized about buying up entire neighbourhoods, including the people in them. But then he was killed in a freak accident. On Highway 11, between Saint Adele and Mount Roland. In his

Lincoln Continental. Instantly decapitated. They searched everywhere, but they never found it.

JOHN What?

BEATRICE His head. They searched the grass on the roadside, and the forest beyond. But they never found the head of the aging gentleman, with its hairpiece and its nearsighted eyes. And my father was not the kind of man to lose his head. I'm his only child. He left me everything. *(She gulps down water.)* But you're letting me do all the talking. What were you asking, before?

JOHN About the reward.

BEATRICE Right, the reward.

JOHN How much?

BEATRICE The biggest paycheque you ever got.

JOHN I prefer cash. Twenty-dollar bills only.

BEATRICE Why?

JOHN It's what I prefer.

BEATRICE But why?

JOHN I like to stack them up in my drawer, or roll them up in my pocket, and then toss them down on the counter, or slip them into a salesman's hand, or give them to kids who ask for "spare change" for coffee.

BEATRICE Fine. I'll pay you in twenties, if you're the successful candidate.

JOHN I'm ready.

BEATRICE For what?

JOHN To get started.

BEATRICE Wait a second. I've got to ask you a few questions, for my archives. What's your name?

JOHN John.

BEATRICE Just "John"?

JOHN   That'll do.

BEATRICE   Age?

JOHN   Put down "Unknown."

BEATRICE   "Unknown"?

JOHN   I can't remember how old I am.

BEATRICE   You must have some idea.

JOHN   Young enough to climb thirty-three floors. Old enough to be winded.

BEATRICE   Fine. Marital status?

JOHN   Alone.

BEATRICE   "Alone"?

JOHN   Alone in my two rooms and a bath, in my bed, alone in my head, in my heart, in my guts.

BEATRICE   Fine. "Alone." Loves?

JOHN   What do you mean, "Loves?"

BEATRICE   How many loves in your life? Before now, I mean?

JOHN   I don't understand the question.

BEATRICE   It's dead simple. How many loves?

JOHN   (after thinking it over) Just write down, "Unknown."

BEATRICE   "Unknown" again?

JOHN   I'm unclear about the definition of "love."

BEATRICE   "The state of wanting only the best for another human being, devoting yourself to her completely."

JOHN   Just write down, "Unknown whether love is measured by volume, by mass, or by speed. Doesn't know the meaning of 'wanting only the best for another human being.' Doesn't know how many loves in his life. Unable to respond to this question."

BEATRICE   All right then. Occupation?

JOHN   Hunter.

BEATRICE   Really? You're my first hunter. So far, I've had a Swedish masseur, a philosophy prof who wrote a thesis on seduction called: "The Temptation of Others," and an expert in water recycling who was the most depressed person I ever met.

JOHN   So, when do we—?

BEATRICE   Then there was a semiologist at the end of his rope— and a well-known actor, who played The Little Green Sprout in those commercials—

JOHN   When can we get—?

BEATRICE   A pizza delivery boy—but only because he got the wrong address—and an ex-con who was selling leather wallets.

JOHN   I'd like to get started.

BEATRICE   Not one of them made it to the second challenge. I sent them all away. Most of them didn't even make it as far as you have. They bored me. I hate being bored. But I don't want to discourage you. So, hunter, what do you hunt? Rabbits, buffalo, butterflies?

JOHN   Rewards.

BEATRICE   Rewards?

JOHN   I'm a bounty hunter. I find missing children and stolen goods, jewellery misplaced by rich old women. I'll do anything to get a reward.

BEATRICE   And do you always get one?

JOHN   Not always.

BEATRICE   What happens when you fail?

JOHN   I go home. I throw up in frustration.

BEATRICE   We're nearly done. These last questions are more personal. What is your principal interest in life?

JOHN   Twenty-dollar bills.

BEATRICE   Nothing else?

JOHN   You said my "principal interest."

BEATRICE   How about a secondary interest?

JOHN   My secondary interest is what you can buy with twenty-dollar bills. Things, services, smiles.

> *BEATRICE nearly smiles, but then goes back to her questions.*

BEATRICE   After dinner, how do you spend your evenings?

JOHN   I go out, I walk the streets, fondling the twenty-dollar bills in my pocket.

BEATRICE   And later?

JOHN   Later, I sleep.

BEATRICE   Do you have nightmares?

JOHN   I dream that someone is slicing me open with a chainsaw.

BEATRICE   And what do they discover, inside you?

JOHN   Absolutely nothing.

BEATRICE   What's the first thing you think of, when you wake up?

JOHN   I think, "I've got to earn some twenty-dollar bills today."

BEATRICE   And later?

JOHN   Later, I search through the newspaper for pictures of girls who are missing, or descriptions of chainsaw killers.

BEATRICE   And if there's nothing interesting in the newspaper?

JOHN   Then I check out the posters on telephone poles, poodles misplaced by rich old women, well-to-do young heiresses who want to be seduced.

BEATRICE   Okay, that's enough. I'm tired. Let's take a break.

JOHN   You need a break?

BEATRICE   That's how I am. I get tired all of a sudden, just like that.

JOHN   I'm anxious to get started.

BEATRICE   Sorry, but I...

> *All of a sudden, BEATRICE falls asleep. JOHN looks at her. He lights up and smokes. He paces. He stops. He paces some more.*
>
> *Outside the wrap-around window, the setting is transformed. From now on, each time BEATRICE falls asleep, the window will suddenly look out on a different landscape – maybe a desert, or the sea, or a rainstorm, or a snowstorm, or the blinding sun, or the dead of night.*
>
> *After a while, BEATRICE wakes up.*

I'm thirsty!

JOHN   So, can we start now?

BEATRICE   Have you ever seen the Nevada desert?

JOHN   No.

BEATRICE   It's inside my mouth. Look. *(She opens her mouth.)*

JOHN   Can we start now?

BEATRICE   I'm thirsty.

> *JOHN brings her a bottle of water. She drinks thirstily.*

If I were you, I'd take a few seconds to pull myself together.

JOHN   Not necessary.

BEATRICE   All right then.

> *JOHN moves to his suitcase, opens it, and begins to unpack.*

I'd better tell you the rules.

JOHN What rules?

BEATRICE The rules of the first challenge.

JOHN Go ahead.

BEATRICE You have to interest me.

JOHN I know that.

BEATRICE To interest me a lot.

JOHN Right.

BEATRICE You have to tell me a story which captures my imagination completely.

JOHN Right.

BEATRICE You think that's going to be easy?

JOHN I don't think anything.

BEATRICE I've personally lived through thousands of wild stories. So yours had better be truly – exceptional.

JOHN "Exceptional"?

BEATRICE Surprise me. I want to hang on your every word.

JOHN "To hang…"?

BEATRICE Like this. *(She sits in front of him and stares, as though hypnotized.)* And then, I must beg you to go on with the story. Three times.

JOHN Okay. Is that it?

BEATRICE You have fifteen minutes. *(She takes out an electronic timer.)*

JOHN Not much time.

BEATRICE Those are the rules.

JOHN Good enough.

> JOHN *goes back to his suitcase, and opens it.*
> *He stares and thinks hard. The moment he begins*
> *speaking, he is transformed: mobile, lively, genial.*

He smiles (his first smile since entering BEATRICE's room).

This is the story of a boy.

BEATRICE activates the timer.

BEATRICE   We've started!

JOHN   A poor boy, born in a shack by the railway tracks on a freezing February night.

BEATRICE   I was born during a heat wave. Imagine. So hot that old people were dropping dead in the slums. I remember, my father told me—

JOHN   When the story begins, the boy is still inside his mother, who is only a girl herself, eighteen years old, huddled up all alone, in this shack by the railway tracks. He is trying to escape from his mother's belly, but she holds him back. She's scared. For nine months she's been scared to death—

BEATRICE   You want to know how I was conceived?

JOHN   For nine months she's been scared to death of what is growing inside her.

BEATRICE   John Dutrisac took his wife Desdemona on a holiday way down South. He checked them into a suite on the top floor of the Coconut Inn. Three days later, there was a severe weather warning. Around midnight, the wind reached hurricane strength. They stood in front of the big bay window and watched the crashing of fifteen-foot waves, and palm trees torn out by the roots, and, all of a sudden—

JOHN   In the shack by the railways tracks, this thing is pushing its way out of the girl's belly, and she is so scared, but she knows she can't hold it back forever, so she opens her legs, and she pushes too—

BEATRICE   All of a sudden, John threw Desdemona down on the carpet, tore off her see-through nightie, and came into her. And, at the exact moment when John Dutrisac spent his seed in the womb of his wife Desdemona, the entire roof of the Coconut Inn was blown off! You heard me, blown off! They were found beneath the wreckage two days later. Newspapers all over the world carried the same headline, "Couple Miraculously Survives Hurricane Beatrice." That's how I was conceived. What do you say to that?

> *JOHN looks at the electronic timer, then continues his story, more emphatically.*

JOHN Like I said, this girl is in a shack by the railway tracks, and this thing is pushing through her, with unimaginable force, like a hurricane—

BEATRICE My mother, the former Desdemona Hilliard—

JOHN So she pushes too and her son slides out between her legs and she picks him up and holds him to her breast and suddenly she screams. Because she just felt something, you see, something like a bee sting underneath her left breast. She examines her newborn son's hands—

BEATRICE My mother, Desdemona, died screaming as I came sliding out of her belly and—

JOHN She examines his left hand and finds nothing, but when she examines his right hand she finds.... She finds... (*He moves to his suitcase and takes something out.*) She finds that her son has something in his right hand. Do you know what her son has in his right hand?

BEATRICE No idea. But my mother died in a pool of blood screaming out my name. My father told me all about it.

JOHN In his right hand, in the steel vice of his tiny fingers, he has... a tiny knife with a leather handle and a razor-sharp blade.

> *JOHN shows BEATRICE the knife he took from his suitcase. Silence.*

BEATRICE A knife?

JOHN A knife. Terrified, the young mother tries to open her newborn son's hand, to make him drop it. But she can't. The baby's fist is like a vice-around the tiny leather handle. Like this. See?

JOHN shows her how firmly his hand is wrapped around the knife handle.

For the first few months, the young mother tries everything to get rid of the knife. She tries to slip it out with soap and with baby oil. She tugs away at the tiny fingers whenever she can. Then, to calm herself down, she says, "As he grows, the little knife will naturally slip through his fingers." But as the boy grows, the knife grows with him.

JOHN moves closer to BEATRICE. She retreats.

Then he's two years old, four years old, eight years old. With the knife in his hand he carves out emptiness all around him. His own mother is afraid to come close. She serves his meals at arms' length.

BEATRICE   *(keeping her distance)* In my case, it was my maid Janine who was afraid of me.

JOHN   *(moving closer to her)* Then he's ten, then twelve. The other boys don't dare come close.

BEATRICE   *(keeping her distance)* I talked to Janine all day, I went shopping with her just so I could continue to converse. Even at night, I woke her up so I could go on talking.

JOHN glances at the timer.

JOHN   Then, when he's fourteen, he feels something being transmitted from the knife, all along his arm, up to his neck and his jaw. A sort of tension.

BEATRICE   What sort of tension?

JOHN   He goes out at night and walks the dark streets with his knife in plain sight pointing the way.

BEATRICE   Why?

JOHN   "Why?" At sixteen, he starts to ask himself, "Why was I born with a knife in my hand? To cut something? To kill somebody?" He walks the streets muttering this question to himself.

JOHN circles BEATRICE.

And then… then one day he sees a girl with long hair, all the way down to her waist, with her maid tip-toeing along behind her. The girl is talking and talking to the maid, who is listening from behind a pile of packages. All of a sudden, the boy knows that the knife is for her. From the start, the knife was for this girl…

He continues circling BEATRICE.

And so he rushes up to the girl who can't stop talking—

He rushes up to BEATRICE with his knife pointed at her.

He grabs her and takes her away, in the middle of the afternoon, he takes her to the edge of the city, to a shack close to the railway tracks.

He keeps his knife pointed at her.

She says, "Stop, get away from me, you've got no right." She can't stop talking. He shouts at her, "Keep silent!"

BEATRICE   Stop. Get away from me.

JOHN   She just goes on talking with her little pink mouth. So he moves even closer and he tells her, "Now you're going to listen to me." He tells her, "You see this knife in my hand? It's been there since the day I was born. I never knew why. But now I know. It's to cut into the mouth of a girl like you. Understand?" Now he pricks the corner of her mouth with the point of the knife.

He raises his knife to BEATRICE's lips. Terrified, she doesn't move.

It's at that exact moment that she understands… she knows exactly what she must do, to save her mouth.

He pauses. BEATRICE doesn't move.

BEATRICE   What must she do, to save her mouth?

JOHN does not respond. He keeps his knife pointed at BEATRICE.

Go on.

JOHN   Go on?

BEATRICE   Go on... with the story.

> *JOHN says nothing.*

Go on with the story. Please.

> *JOHN takes one step back and plants himself in front of BEATRICE. He stares at her. Sitting on the edge of her chair, she is "hanging on his every word," just as she specified at the start. The electronic timer beeps, his time is up. JOHN grabs the Polaroid camera and takes a photo of BEATRICE. She snaps out of her trance.*

JOHN   Success.

BEATRICE   You – you cheated!

JOHN   No, I didn't.

BEATRICE   You had a knife.

JOHN   You never said knives aren't allowed.

BEATRICE   No, but—

JOHN   Success.

> *BEATRICE shudders.*

BEATRICE   I'm cold.

JOHN   You were hanging on my every word.

BEATRICE   Don't you think it's cold in here?

JOHN   So, we go on to the second challenge?

BEATRICE   I'm – I'm tired.

JOHN   Not again!

> *BEATRICE falls asleep. JOHN watches her. Outside the window a new landscape appears. After a moment, BEATRICE wakes up.*

BEATRICE   I'm thirsty.

JOHN brings her a bottle of water. She drinks.

I need the ocean.

JOHN   Why?

BEATRICE   To wash away all the sand inside. Look.

She opens her mouth.

JOHN   So, do we go on?

BEATRICE   What did she have to do, to save her mouth?

JOHN   Do we go on now?

BEATRICE   She had to seduce him, right? Or she had to kiss his hand and beg forgiveness? Or give him a reward?

JOHN   Remind me of the rules.

BEATRICE   Or she had to keep silent? She had to promise to keep silent forever? Answer me.

JOHN   Can we go on?

BEATRICE   I want the knife.

JOHN   All right.

He gives her the knife.

BEATRICE   And I want to see what else is in your suitcase.

JOHN   Impossible.

BEATRICE   Why?

JOHN   Because that's how it is. But I promise you there are no more knives. You have my word on that. So, do we go on now?

Pause. BEATRICE looks at him for a long time.

BEATRICE   I have to tell you...

JOHN   What?

BEATRICE   Nothing.

JOHN   Tell me about the second challenge. What do I have to do?

BEATRICE   There's no point. You'll never succeed.

JOHN   Let me try.

BEATRICE   But I'm... I'm so tired.

> *She closes her eyes. Outside the window, a slight change of landscape.*

JOHN   No, you don't. Stand up. Walk around.

> *He gets her to her feet and walks her around energetically.*

I have to *move* you, isn't that it?

BEATRICE   Yes—move me—but it won't be easy. Practically impossible, in fact.

JOHN   Why will it be impossible?

BEATRICE   Because I lack humidity. I read somewhere that emotions germinate in humidity. Like mushrooms.

JOHN   So how do I do it?

BEATRICE   That's for you to discover.

JOHN   Okay, so I have to move you – but how far?

BEATRICE   To tears.

JOHN   How many tears?

BEATRICE   Till my cheeks glisten.

JOHN   What's the time limit?

BEATRICE   Same as before.

JOHN   Not very much.

BEATRICE   And this time you can't force me. Tears can't be forced.

JOHN   Then, this time, you're going to listen to me.

BEATRICE   Why?

JOHN   Because that's the rule. I agree to the time limit, and you agree to keep silent and watch me. Just watch me. Okay?

BEATRICE   All right. But I'm warning you, if I get bored—

JOHN   Can I start now?

> BEATRICE looks at him, thinks about it, then she traces an imaginary line on the floor, and places her armchair on one side of the line. She sits.

BEATRICE   Okay. But you can't step over that line.

JOHN   All right.

> She drinks a big gulp of water, then starts the electronic timer.

BEATRICE   Begin!

> JOHN goes to his suitcase and takes out two marionettes, one larger than the other.

What are you doing?

> JOHN performs a marionette show.

JOHN   This is the story of a little boy who is scared of the dark...

LITTLE BOY   (the smaller marionette, as though awakening from a nightmare) Oh! I'm scared! I'm scared!

JOHN   And his grandfather who makes a lot of noise when he breathes.

GRANDFATHER   (the larger marionette, making a lot of noise when he breathes) Don't be scared, my child.

BEATRICE   When I was little, my father took me to the zoo and what scared me were the lions and tigers and panthers—

> JOHN stops the puppet show and looks at her.

Okay. I'll keep silent.

JOHN   (*continuing his show*) The little boy and his grandfather, who makes a lot of noise when he breathes, spend one week every summer in the country where they try to catch catfish. All day long they fish in silence. Sometimes the little boy starts talking.

LITTLE BOY   Catfish are very smart, aren't they, Grandpa?

GRANDFATHER   Ssshh! No talking. We'll scare the catfish.

JOHN   So the little boy keeps silent. And the grandfather breathes noisily. In the evening they play cards, and after four hands of "Go Fish" the grandfather turns out the light.

GRANDFATHER   Okay. Sleepy Time. The catfish have already gone to bed. They're resting up for tomorrow.

LITTLE BOY   Oh no! Not yet! One more hand, please, just one more hand!

BEATRICE   When I was little, my father told me the story of some children who got lost and—

JOHN stops the show.

Okay, okay. I'll keep silent.

JOHN   The little boy wants to play another hand, but Grandpa won't hear of it. He leads the little boy to their big bed. It's all dark in the cabin and the little boy is very scared. To calm himself down, he counts the seconds between Grandpa's noisy breaths.

LITTLE BOY   One, two, three...

GRANDFATHER breathes noisily.

One, two, three...

GRANDFATHER breathes noisily.

One, two, three...

GRANDFATHER breathes noisily.

JOHN   Sometime during their seventh night at the cabin, the little boy dreams that he's fighting a duel with a monster catfish.

LITTLE BOY   Take that, you filthy catfish!

JOHN   He wakes up with a start. He's scared of the dark. Automatically he starts counting the seconds until his grandfather breathes again.

LITTLE BOY   One, two, three…

JOHN   But he hears nothing.

LITTLE BOY   Five, six, seven, eight…

JOHN   Still nothing.

LITTLE BOY   Fifteen, sixteen, seventeen, eighteen…

JOHN   He goes on counting in the darkness. At exactly two-hundred-and-forty-three, he knows that he is all alone with a corpse in the big cold bed.

> *Pause. JOHN seems moved.*

At four-hundred-and-seventy-two, he closes his grandfather's eyes. At eight-hundred-and-fifty-three, he sits up in bed. At ten-thousand-five-hundred-and-forty, the sun comes up. At fifteen-thousand-eight-hundred-and-eighty-three, he steps out onto the front porch. At exactly sixteen-thousand-six-hundred, he begins to vomit on the red and white petunias planted around the stairs. He vomits up the catfish which he ate for supper, and the potatoes and peas, and the chocolate-chip cookies, and his fear of the dark, and his nightmares of monster fish who excel at fencing, and his entire terrified childhood. At eighteen-thousand-seven-hundred-and-seventy-eight, he starts walking toward the village. At nineteen-thousand-three-hundred-and-eighty-two, a truck pulls up beside him. The driver asks, "Are you all alone, little boy?" He says, "Yes, I am all alone."

> *Pause.*

He's eight years old. He understands that you can't count on somebody else's breathing to keep you alive.

> *Pause. BEATRICE raises one hand to her face.*

You're crying.

BEATRICE   No, I'm not. Feel my face, it's dry. Stories about little boys who are scared of the dark never make me cry.

> *She moves closer to him. She reaches out across the imaginary line on the floor and touches his cheek.*

JOHN   Okay. I'll go on.

BEATRICE   *(looking at the timer)* You're almost out of time.

JOHN   Right.

> *He searches for another idea.*

So the little boy grows up. He's a man now. It's night time, and he comes home.

> *JOHN goes to the door and acts as though he's just entered.*

He does nothing for a moment, then he lights a small lamp. Then he looks at his feet.

> *JOHN looks down. Silence.*

BEATRICE   So what? A man looks at his feet.

JOHN   I'll start again. It's night time. He comes home. He's cold. He shivers.

> *He enacts the scene.*

He lights a small lamp.

> *He goes to the window.*

He's all alone. There's not a sound. He looks down. He shivers.

> *He looks. He shivers.*

BEATRICE   Some man shivers. So what?

JOHN   I'll start again. It's night time. He comes home. He's… he's soaking wet.

> *He grabs a bottle of water and pours it over his head.*

He's cold.

He shivers.

He goes to the window. He looks down. He sits down. He counts the seconds between his own breaths. One, two, three.... One, two, three.... One, two, three, four, five, six.... One, two, three, four, five, six, seven, eight…

BEATRICE   Stop. Time's up.

JOHN   I didn't hear the beeper.

BEATRICE   The batteries must be shot. But your time is definitely up.

JOHN   One, two, three, four, five, six, seven, eight, nine, ten, eleven—

BEATRICE   Stop.

JOHN   He counts until he runs out of breath. One, two, three, four, five…

His breathing becomes shaky.

BEATRICE   Stop.

JOHN   He counts and his shoulders begin to shake.

> *JOHN reproduces the breathing of someone who is weeping. BEATRICE watches him. This lasts for a while. JOHN's suffering seems more and more real. BEATRICE raises a hand to her face. Pause.*

You're crying.

BEATRICE   No, I'm not. I've got something in my eye.

> *JOHN moves closer. He grabs a bottle of water, pours some onto his hands, then touches BEATRICE's face.*

JOHN   Now you're crying.

> *He caresses her face with his wet hands.*

You're crying.

> *BEATRICE dries her face with her hands. JOHN touches her face. He stares at her. Then he moves away. He takes her picture with the Polaroid camera.*

> *BEATRICE snatches the camera away from him and throws it down.*

Success.

> *BEATRICE says nothing.*

You were moved. I saw it in your eyes.

> *BEATRICE says nothing.*

I passed the second challenge.

> *BEATRICE says nothing.*

BEATRICE   No. You cheated. I…. Excuse me.

> *BEATRICE falls asleep. JOHN shakes her.*

JOHN   No. No sleeping. You put up a poster. You promised a "substantial reward." We're going on.

BEATRICE   I'm thirsty.

JOHN   I don't give a shit. We're going on.

BEATRICE   We're stopping.

JOHN   We're not done.

BEATRICE   Yes, we are. We're stopping.

JOHN   Why?

BEATRICE   Because… I'm tired. Excuse me.

> *She falls asleep. JOHN shakes her.*

JOHN   Wake up.

BEATRICE   Listen, I have to tell you—

JOHN   Tell me about the third challenge.

BEATRICE   There's something I need to tell you.

> *JOHN takes out BEATRICE's poster and summarizes it for her.*

JOHN   "Well-to-do young heiress promises a SUBSTANTIAL REWARD to the man who can interest, move, and *seduce* her." So, what do I have to do to seduce you? And how much time do I have?

BEATRICE   I want to tell you—

JOHN   Should I make you laugh, or at least giggle, make you blush a little, is that it? What's your idea of being seduced?

BEATRICE   I have to tell you… about my maid Janine.

JOHN   Should I kiss your hand? Whatever I have to do—

BEATRICE   She never listened to me. I never woke her up in the middle of the night to talk to her, but—

JOHN   You have to lie down and spread your legs, and I have to lie down on you, and you have to wind your fingers through my hair, and you have to whisper my name, ever so softly. Is that it?

BEATRICE   Listen to me!

JOHN   Let's get on with it.

BEATRICE   But I wanted to wake her up, don't you understand? I wanted her to listen to me, I wanted somebody to *listen* to me at last. But Janine could never really hear me because…

> *While BEATRICE is talking, JOHN rifles through his suitcase. He takes out a cassette player, and starts a cassette, an operatic duet. BEATRICE raises her voice.*

Because she did not exist.

> *JOHN moves closer to BEATRICE, singing along with the tenor.*

And I also need to tell you, as far as my fourteen lovers go—

> *JOHN reaches out for her, emoting comically.*

What are you doing? Stop that.

> *She laughs, or at least giggles. JOHN sings louder. She laughs louder. He throws himself down on his knees in front of her, singing. They continue this*

game of laughter and seduction. He seizes
BEATRICE's hand.

I'm not sure there were exactly fourteen. Maybe more. Maybe
less. I didn't love them, it's true, but I tried to. I really tried.
I studied them closely, their arms, their jaw lines, their hips.
I cooked them rack of lamb. Somebody told me, "When you
love a man, you cook him rack of lamb." I bought them
evergreen-scented after-shave. Somebody told me, "When
you love a man, you buy him after-shave." I worked hard to
surprise them. I invited them to dinner and received them
wearing nothing but a see-through raincoat. I watched their
eyes grow round and their faces grow red with pleasure.
I hung on their necks and smiled, I welcomed them to my
bed and asked them to tell me stories about when they were
little boys – but I always ended up falling asleep, I was so
tired, I am so tired. But I let them lie down on me, and
I made all the expected noises. Somebody told me, "When
you love a man, you're expected to scream..."

JOHN kisses her hand.

What are you doing?

JOHN places BEATRICE's hand on his heart.

Stop now. Stop that. I'm tired, so tired.

She falls asleep. JOHN bends over BEATRICE and
breathes on her face. She wakes up.

JOHN Show me.

BEATRICE What?

JOHN How you hung on the necks of your fourteen lovers.

He immediately helps BEATRICE to her feet, then
places her arms around his neck. She stays that way.

Like that? And then what did they do? Did they take your
face between their hands like this?

He takes BEATRICE's face between his hands.

Did they say you have beautiful eyes? Did they describe your face? The sweet hollows beneath your cheekbones, your magnificent hair? Did they say, "You're like no one else in the world. I never met anyone like you. I never saw such fear, such fire in another glance, such sadness, such anger in another face. I want to hold you like this forever. I want to offer you—something—everything"!

BEATRICE   No, they – they didn't say that.

JOHN   "I never saw skin like yours before, a mouth like yours. So sweet outside, but dry as the Sahara inside. I want to explore it, plunge through the sand and discover a source of fresh water, an oasis shaded by palm trees."

> *He gently explores BEATRICE's mouth with*
> *a finger.*

BEATRICE   They never said that.

JOHN   Show me.

BEATRICE   What?

JOHN   How you welcomed them to your bed.

BEATRICE   Let's stop. Okay?

JOHN   Show me how they told you their little boy stories.

> *He reaches out to BEATRICE. She doesn't move.*

BEATRICE   I have to tell you something…

JOHN   Come here.

> *She doesn't move. He comes closer. He pulls*
> *her forward.*

Come here. Sit down.

> *He gently forces her to sit.*

BEATRICE   My mother didn't die giving birth to me in a pool of blood. Not exactly.

JOHN   Did they caress your hair as they talked?

> *He caresses her hair.*

BEATRICE   And her name wasn't Desdemona. But it could have been. With her magnificent hair. And her skin. She could have been called Desdemona.

JOHN   When I was ten, I used to kiss the girls on television. I used to press my lips to the TV screen. It was so cold. Are you listening to me?

He kisses her delicately.

BEATRICE   No. I'm tired. Sorry, I—

She sleeps. JOHN bends over and gently awakens her.

JOHN   Listen to me, Beatrice. I kissed the TV screen. It was so cold. But I could feel the softness of their lips. I could even smell their perfume. The waxy scent of their lipstick. I heard them murmuring my name. "John. John." I kissed them. Come and lie down.

He helps her lie down on the floor.

BEATRICE   My mother died, when I was very young, of a brain disease. No longer able to remember her own name.

JOHN   Let me lie down on you, Beatrice.

He delicately opens her legs. She closes them.

BEATRICE   At night in my bedroom, I used to talk to her photograph. I asked her all about angels, and dragons, and eternity. She was smiling in her photograph.

JOHN   Let me lie down on you.

He opens her legs. She closes them again.

BEATRICE   I'm not sure if I loved her. Can you love a photograph? What does it mean, to love your mother? I'm so tired.

JOHN   "Let me." Is that what they said to you? "Please, let me. Let me lie down on you."

He opens her legs again. She doesn't close them.
He lies down on her.

What did you say to them, when they lay down on you?

BEATRICE   Nothing. I said nothing. I'm tired.

JOHN   You must have said their names, very softly. Say it, say my name, Beatrice. Say it with me, "John."

> *BEATRICE says nothing. JOHN kisses her face.*

Say it. Please. It's easy. Try it, "John."

BEATRICE   *(faintly)* I don't know… I'm…

> *She sleeps. JOHN gently wakes her up.*

JOHN   Say it, please. Say it with me, "John."

> *He kisses her hair, her neck, her shoulders. He lays his ear against BEATRICE's lips.*

Say it.

> *BEATRICE murmurs something inaudible.*

Again.

> *BEATRICE again murmurs in JOHN's ear.*

Again, say it again, with me, "John, John, John."

> *BEATRICE murmurs again in JOHN's ear. They stay like this for a long moment. BEATRICE touches JOHN's face. They look at one another, for a long time. They don't move. Finally, JOHN stands and goes to his suitcase.*

Pay me.

> *BEATRICE says nothing.*

You've been seduced. Pay me.

BEATRICE   I…. That's not… being seduced.

JOHN   So, what is being seduced?

BEATRICE   Something stronger, like a flood in the desert in the middle of July.

JOHN   A flood? There are no floods. There are just bodies, and smiles, and whispers, and hands touching faces. Success.

BEATRICE   I need to tell you—

JOHN   You listened, you were captivated, your cheeks glistened, you smiled, you blushed, you opened your legs.

BEATRICE   But that wasn't real.

JOHN   What's "real"?

BEATRICE   I don't know for sure, but it's more than that. More tension, more emotion, more desire, more trembling, more certainty, more, more, more.

JOHN   Trembling? Certainty? You never said anything about "certainty."

BEATRICE   I want to tell you—

JOHN   You put up a poster.

BEATRICE   Yes, I put a poster on every telephone pole in the city. It was raining and I was so cold.

JOHN   You put up a poster promising a "substantial reward."

BEATRICE   I had been sitting here for weeks, in this armchair, drinking water to drown the sand inside me and the little dead branches and rocks and the withered cactus. Then, one night, I took a sheet of paper and I wrote, "Well-to-do young heiress, intelligent and perceptive—"

JOHN   Pay me.

BEATRICE   "Well-to-do young heiress, intelligent and perceptive, who has never loved anyone, neither her mother nor her father, nor her cat..." I never had a cat. I had a rabbit. My father gave me one, but I didn't love it. What does it mean, to love a rabbit...?

JOHN   I don't want to know whether you loved your rabbit, I want you to—

BEATRICE   I wrote, "Well-to-do young heiress is seeking a man who will *interest*, *move*, and *seduce* her." Somebody told me, "When you love a man, then you don't think so much about all the things that hurt you, like the passing of time, and the truth which is never really the truth."

JOHN   Listen. It's not a question of—

BEATRICE   It was raining. I went out with my stack of posters, a can of glue and a paintbrush. I began by gluing my posters to telephone poles, then to fences, then to the doors of houses.

JOHN   I said listen. It was never a question of loving anybody or anything. It was a question of three challenges and a "substantial reward."

BEATRICE   Then I came back up here. I was soaking wet. I dried off. I waited. Some men stopped by and I sent them on their way. Then you arrived. You say you've succeeded, but I don't think—

JOHN   You don't think what?…

BEATRICE   I am still thinking about all the things which hurt me.

JOHN   Everybody thinks about what hurts them. That doesn't change anything. Pay me.

　　　　　　　Pause.

BEATRICE   I want to tell you—

JOHN   What? What now?

BEATRICE   My father was not John Dutrisac—

JOHN   I don't give a shit. Pay me.

BEATRICE   Not the famous plastic garbage can king. He sold insurance. His name was George.

JOHN   Okay, so his name was George, but I don't—

BEATRICE   He didn't lose his head on Highway 11. He didn't have a hairpiece and he wasn't nearsighted.

JOHN   And I need to know this because…?

BEATRICE   He had tiny mean eyes. He did once buy an old building. He was in debt up to his eyes when he died, of an embolism in his brain, while playing high-stakes poker. He left me—

JOHN   I know, the whole street from the souvlaki place to the gay bar—

BEATRICE   He left me his beat-up old Chevrolet and the mortgage—

JOHN   The mortgage?

BEATRICE   On this one old building, plus all the rest of his debts.

JOHN   What are you telling me?

BEATRICE   I don't have a cent.

JOHN   What?

BEATRICE   I can't pay you anything…

>   *Pause.*

JOHN   Say it again.

BEATRICE   I can't pay you. No paycheque. No twenty-dollar bills.

JOHN   You can't be serious.

BEATRICE   It's the truth.

JOHN   You put up a poster, you make me climb all the way up here, thirty-three flights, no elevator—

BEATRICE   Sorry about the elevator.

JOHN   You let me in, I ask you, "How much?" you tell me about your father, again I ask you, "How much?" you tell me about his head on Highway 11—

BEATRICE   That image came to me spontaneously—

JOHN   You tell me about the three challenges, you quote me the rules, I succeed, and when it's time to pay up, you say you can't pay me anything. That's not possible. It can't go like that, understand?

BEATRICE   But I don't—

JOHN   It can't go like that. You can't work it that way, understand? You promised. We had a deal.

BEATRICE   But now I'm telling you—

JOHN   I succeeded. I want something. Give me something!

BEATRICE   What do you want?

JOHN   I want my "substantial reward"!

>   *He shakes her.*

BEATRICE   Everything I've got is right here. Look around. You want some apples? You want water? You want the armchair? Take it. You want the men who came before you, the philosopher, the engineer, the semiologist at the end of his rope, the actor, the pizza boy, the ex-con? Take them.

>   *She tears the photos down from the wall and gives them to him. He tosses them aside.*

JOHN   You wrote "SUBSTANTIAL REWARD."

BEATRICE   I know what I wrote.

JOHN   I want something.

BEATRICE   You want a story? My true story? I was conceived one November evening. My father was named Roger, my mother, Louise. They made me while watching a hurricane on the ten o'clock news.

JOHN   I don't want a story, I want something concrete, something I can touch, can take between my hands, something I can shove into my pocket—

BEATRICE   Like what? My shirt? Take it.

>   *She takes off her shirt and gives it to him.*
>   *He throws it down.*

You want my shoes? My twenty-dollar necklace?

>   *She takes off her shoes and the little chain she wears around her neck. She gives them to him. He tosses them aside.*

What do you want? My hair? My long hair like a Medieval princess? Take it.

She takes off her long hair and throws it at him. He picks it up, stunned.

You can cut it up, shove it into your pocket, and walk the streets, saying to yourself, "I won. I passed all three challenges." You can mount it over your fireplace like a trophy. You can sell it, if you want to. Go on, take it, it's all I've got.

JOHN stands for a long moment, without moving, with BEATRICE's long hair in his hands.

JOHN   But what can I—?

BEATRICE   Somebody told me, "A woman waiting for a man should have long hair all the way down to her waist."

JOHN   What do you want me to say?

BEATRICE   Somebody told me, "When you love a man, then you don't have to think so much about death, and you don't feel all dried up inside." I asked them, "But what does it mean, to love a man?" They told me, "To be interested, moved, seduced." So I put up a poster. I promised a "substantial reward."

JOHN   Why? If you have nothing to give?

BEATRICE   Somebody told me, "A man needs to be offered a substantial reward, so that he can meet the challenges."

JOHN   That's ridiculous.

BEATRICE   Would you have come if I'd offered nothing?

JOHN   Of course not.

BEATRICE   You see?

JOHN   I want something.

BEATRICE   I've given you all I have.

JOHN   Right. I'm out of here.

BEATRICE   No!

JOHN   Why not?

BEATRICE   Don't go yet.

JOHN   You made a promise. You didn't keep it. You lied. I'm out of here.

BEATRICE   Stay for a minute.

JOHN   You make me climb up here. You propose some challenges, and when you see that I'm winning, you want to stop, and now that I want to go, you want me to stay. What's wrong with you?

BEATRICE   I don't want to sit and stare out the window anymore.

JOHN   I'm out of here. Give me the key.

BEATRICE   You took me in your arms, you lay down on me.

JOHN   Only because—

BEATRICE   For the reward, I know. But I almost heard you and I almost cried. It wasn't really real, but maybe it was the beginning—

JOHN   The beginning of what?

BEATRICE   I don't know. Maybe it begins like this, "There are two people in the room—"

JOHN   "There are two people in the room, and one of them wants to clear out, and the other one has the key but no 'substantial reward.'" That's a great beginning!

BEATRICE   "There are two of them in the room now, which is better than sitting alone in front of the only window."

JOHN   Who says? Who says it's better?

BEATRICE   What do you think? That it's better to throw up alone in two rooms and a bath? It's better to lock the door and stagger to the bathroom and throw up all the loss which makes us sick to our stomachs?

JOHN   What loss?

BEATRICE   Everything we've lost, which we miss so much, without being able to say what it is.

JOHN   I don't know what you're talking about.

BEATRICE   Oh yes, you do.

JOHN   I've got to get out of here.

BEATRICE   No. Stay.

JOHN   Give me the key.

> *He rushes toward her. She brandishes the knife.*

BEATRICE   Not yet.

JOHN   Let me out.

BEATRICE   Don't go. Not yet.

JOHN   You really think you can stop me from going?

> *She runs away. He tries to grab her. She keeps the knife pointed at him. She runs to the window. She looks all around, then out the window. She takes the key from over her heart, and holds it tightly in one hand.*
>
> *He moves closer. She opens the single functional pane of the large window. Noise of the city invades the room. He moves closer still. She throws the key out into space, then closes the pane.*
>
> *JOHN and BEATRICE stare out the window for a long time, as if searching for the key on the sidewalk, thirty-three floors down. Then they look at one another, and all around, realizing that they are locked inside this room.*

What did—? Why did you—? What did you—?

BEATRICE   I'm thirsty.

JOHN   Why did you do that?

BEATRICE   I'm thirsty.

JOHN goes to the door, tries to force it open.

JOHN   I want out of here!

BEATRICE   Nobody's getting out.

JOHN   There must be another key.

BEATRICE   No, there's not.

JOHN   You're crazy. You're totally crazy.

BEATRICE   No. I'm not crazy.

JOHN   You locked us in.

BEATRICE   Have a drink of water.

She hands him a bottle of water.

JOHN   I don't want a drink, I want to leave.

BEATRICE   You want to, but you can't.

JOHN   Fuck!

He turns in a circle, looking at the room.

Now what do we do? Huh? What do we do now?

BEATRICE   Now...

JOHN   We lose our minds, is that it? We're locked in, so we lose our minds.

She puts the knife down on the floor between them.

BEATRICE   Now we're locked in, so we... we love one another.

JOHN sniggers.

JOHN   "We love one another"? What does that mean, to "love one another"?

BEATRICE   I'm not sure. We have to find out.

JOHN   Look at me. Look at my face, my eyes, my mouth. What do you see?

BEATRICE looks at him.

BEATRICE   I see… your face, your eyes, your mouth.

JOHN   And, behind them, do you see a little flame?

BEATRICE   I see…. Um…

JOHN   No. You don't see a little flame because there isn't one. And the word "Love" is not engraved somewhere inside my head. You could explore my mouth, descend into my chest with a flashlight, check out all the caves inside me 'til you run out of air, and you won't find anything. Not even a little inscription which says, "I am here," "John is here." Not even the shape of a heart scratched on the walls. Not even a little stick figure who's crying. Nothing. I'm a bounty hunter. I came here to be challenged and to get—

BEATRICE   Your reward, I know.

JOHN   I don't know anything about "loving one another."

BEATRICE   Neither do I. But we could look.

JOHN   You can't look for something if you don't know what it is.

BEATRICE   You don't know what it is, but when you find it, you'll recognize it. It's weird, but that's how it is—

JOHN   Ridiculous.

>   *Pause.*

BEATRICE   We could start by telling each other something true. Somebody told me, "When you love someone, you tell them the truth." You go first.

>   *JOHN says nothing.*

Okay, I'll go first. My father… my real father was named Gavin, and my mother was named Yvonne, and they made me one spring day in a motel room when it wasn't raining at all and…. No. That's not true. Um…. I was born, I grew up and became a little girl and then I became a woman. A woman who's locked in here. A woman who threw the key away, who's thirsty, who's sick to her stomach, and who wants to love someone. Yes, that's true. I think that's true. Now it's your turn. You tell me something true.

JOHN says nothing.

What was your father's name? Tell me that much at least. What was his real name?

JOHN says nothing.

Okay. Then tell me about your work. Men love to talk about their work.

JOHN says nothing.

How did you become a bounty hunter, John?

JOHN   You don't want to know.

BEATRICE   Sure, I do. I'm dying to know.

JOHN   Okay. One day, a long time ago, I was walking along a riverbank. I heard somebody screaming. I saw an arm waving above a huge whirlpool. I dived in. The water was like ice. I had to swim against the current. It was so hard.

BEATRICE   But how did you become—?

JOHN   Wait. Let me finish. When I arrived at the whirlpool, there was only one hand above the water. As soon as I touched it, it grabbed onto me. I pulled for all I was worth. A head appeared. I wrapped my arm around the neck. I swam back to the riverbank dragging a lifeless body. I stretched the body out on the shore. A young woman's body. I bent over and put my lips to hers, I breathed into her – ten, twenty, thirty times. I lay down on her, trying to share my warmth. Finally she opened her eyes. And – it was like she had saved me. Like it was me who was drowning and she who breathed into my lungs. I can't explain it. Afterwards—several hours later—we got to our feet, we walked to her house. But she had changed. She wasn't the same at all. Her voice was too shrill, her forehead was too high, her dress was too fancy. Days went by. I no longer recognized her. She wasn't the same girl I dragged out of the river. I wanted to go back there, to the whirlpool, to try and feel it again, how our breath mingled. But she wouldn't go. She was afraid. "Never again to that river," she said. Then her father came home after a long trip. When he found out what happened, he said, "You saved my daughter's life. I want to give you a reward." I was going to say, "You don't need to do that," but then I stopped myself. I looked at the girl. I couldn't remember it anymore – her wet body, or the warmth of her breath inside my mouth. I smiled. I said, "I'd be happy to accept." He held out a roll of twenty-dollar bills. I shoved it into my pocket. And I left. That's how I became a bounty hunter.

BEATRICE   Is that the truth?

JOHN   What's the truth? The exact moment when you breathe into a drowned girl's mouth, the mingling of your breath? Or is it the moment when you suddenly notice how shrill her voice is, how fancy her dress is? Or is it the silence between you, which is so terrible, but which eventually becomes your way of life? Or is it the moment when you say to yourself, "Who is this girl? What's she doing in my life?" What's the truth?

BEATRICE   I don't know, but something ought to be true in your story. One thing at least.

JOHN   True. There's one thing. Which is real, concrete, indisputable.

BEATRICE   What's that?

JOHN   The roll of twenties in my pocket. Their shape, their feel, their smell, the delight of touching them. That's true. Everything else passes by you like a breeze. No shape, no consistency. It brushes past you and it's gone.

BEATRICE   But when the breeze blows over you, it's true. It warms you up or it cools you off or it ruffles your hair, but it changes you.

JOHN   If something's true, then it's true. It doesn't turn into something completely different for no reason.

BEATRICE   Okay. Maybe it's too hard, looking for the truth. Let's try something else.

JOHN   Like what?

BEATRICE   I don't know. Making gestures.

JOHN   We've done that. We've used up all the gestures.

BEATRICE   No. There must be others.

> *Pause.*

What are you thinking?

JOHN   I'm thinking that I want to get out of here.

BEATRICE   You can't get out. We're locked in.

> *A long silence. JOHN and BEATRICE have retreated to opposite sides of the room. After a while, BEATRICE moves closer to JOHN and touches his face and his neck.*

JOHN   What are you doing?

BEATRICE   Seeing if you have a fever.

JOHN   Why?

BEATRICE   Because that's what women do. They express love in this simple little gesture.

JOHN   I don't have a fever.

BEATRICE   How do you know?

> *She repeats the gesture delicately.*

JOHN   Do I?

BEATRICE   No. I don't think so.

> *A long silence. BEATRICE moves close to JOHN again. She scratches his back.*

When there are two of you, you can get your back scratched.

> *JOHN lets her.*

JOHN Lower.

> *BEATRICE scratches lower.*

To the right…. No, to the left, and up a little. Yes! There! Aaah…

> *He makes satisfied sounds. BEATRICE bends down in front of him and presents her back. He scratches it without conviction.*

BEATRICE Harder.

> *He scratches harder.*

Harder.

> *He scratches harder.*

Stop – you're hurting me!

> *He stops. Pause.*

JOHN So, is that it?

BEATRICE Is that what?

JOHN Are we loving one another yet?

BEATRICE No. I don't think so.

> *Pause.*

We could try facing one another and just staring—

JOHN Or we could go to sleep. How about that? Close our eyes. Forget that we're here.

BEATRICE Sleep? Yes, you're right. Sleep with our arms around each other. United. I lie down beside you and you hold my hand and I rest my head on your shoulder, and, before we fall asleep, we discuss our aches and pains. For example, I have a pain right here, just above my abdomen. It hurts especially in the morning when I open my eyes and hope for something, no matter what, and then again in the evening when I go to bed and I'm not hoping for anything. It's like a little hand which opens and closes just beneath the skin, right here, it pulls and pulls. I get up and have a drink of water, but it doesn't stop.

Pause.

JOHN   Let me sleep.

BEATRICE   Surely you have an ache or a pain. Somewhere. Everybody does.

JOHN   Let me sleep!

Pause.

BEATRICE   Why won't you talk to me? Talk to me!

JOHN   Sorry, I'm tired. I just get tired all of a sudden, so tired, that's how I am.

BEATRICE   Wake up.

JOHN   Leave me the fuck alone!

Pause. He looks like he's sleeping.

BEATRICE   That's right. We have to fight sometimes. Love is fighting, struggling to get your own way, calling each other names, then falling into each other's arms. I read that somewhere. You ask for something, he says "No," you insist, and you end up having one hell of a fight.

Pause. JOHN still looks like he's sleeping.

Sweetheart, answer me when I talk to you.

JOHN   Leave me alone!

BEATRICE   Why are you always like this? Mr. High-And-Mighty doesn't want to talk. Mr. High-And-Mighty is tired. Mr. High-And-Mighty seals himself up inside his private bubble and floats far above the whole world.

JOHN   What the hell are you talking about?

BEATRICE   If you must know, I'm sick of your attitude. I'm sick of your pretending that you don't know what I'm talking about, as if you just arrived from another planet. You think you're better than me, better than anybody. You think you're exceptional. You're not exceptional. You're just a man who sweats and belches and snores.

JOHN   I never said I was—

BEATRICE   You assume that you're an exceptional human being, who can understand everything in the world, and who can work everything out for himself, and to hell with anybody else who might have a different idea. They'll just have to deal with it. So why don't *you* learn to deal with it, sweetheart? Deal with that persistent little pain in your belly, deal with your meaningless life, I'm tired now, and I've never understood all your babble, and I have an empty cave deep inside me, and, if you want, I'll give you a guided tour, you can see for yourself how deep and dark and cold it is, and you'd better bring along a flashlight because it's going to scare the hell out of you—

JOHN   You're hysterical.

BEATRICE   What?

JOHN   You're actually hysterical. I've never seen that before. The words pouring out like Niagara Falls, never never never stopping. The rest of us have to swim hard to keep from drowning in your ideas, your expectations, your aches and pains. Not to be swallowed up by your questions, your doubts, your lies, your millions of lies piled up on top of one another – you and you and you and you! You take up all the space in this room. Every ounce of oxygen, you guzzle it down, every particle of silence, you swallow it up. You chew it all up and then spit out your hysteria. It spatters all over the walls, the floor, all over me. Shreds of your hysteria all over me, and it's sticky and it stinks and I can't stand it—

BEATRICE   What about you? Moving in your mysterious little ways, your silence, your coldness, you think they don't stick to me? They writhe through the room like snakes through slime, winding around my arms and legs and my neck and chilling me to the—

JOHN   (*raising his hand to strike her*) Stop it! Stop or I'll—

BEATRICE   (*moving closer to JOHN*) Go ahead, hit me, if you're not afraid to. Stop playing Mr. High-And-Mighty for once in your life. Show me what's eating away at you—

JOHN   Don't push me.

> *She pushes him.*

BEATRICE   Go on, show me – your anger, your resentment, your hatred of me.

> *She pushes him again. He hits her. They fight, like lovers sometimes fight. They tear each other's hair, they tear at one another, crying out in shrill strangled voices.*

I hate you.

JOHN   Stop it!

BEATRICE   You're sick.

JOHN   You're crazy, completely crazy. Certifiable.

> *They go on fighting. JOHN gets BEATRICE into a painful arm lock.*

BEATRICE   Ooww! You're hurting me. Stop!

JOHN   Say that I was right. Say that you're so crazy they ought to lock you up.

BEATRICE   Stop, stop, stop!

> *She screams as loud as she can and goes on struggling. He lets her go. They remain face to face, out of breath, trembling. They move to their separate corners and sit, exhausted. A long pause. BEATRICE stands and moves to JOHN.*

I'm sorry. I – didn't mean to say those things. Take me in your arms. Please.

> *She goes to him and slides into JOHN's arms delicately.*

We got carried away. Now we make up, right? That's the best part, making up after a fight. You feel so small and fragile and you understand how you'd hate to lose one another. Yes?

>   *JOHN says nothing.*

You say, "I should never have let it go that far, the words just poured out of me, how can I explain?" and I say, "No, no, it was all my fault, you were only—"

JOHN   And then we keep silent.

BEATRICE   That's right. It's better not to talk. We listen to our hearts beating. We think about those things which please us, in spite of everything, about one another, like… I don't know.… Um.… Your arms, so strong and warm, and also—

JOHN   We keep silent and we think about how ridiculous it all is. We realize that we mean nothing to each other, that we never meant anything, and we've just been pretending all along.

>   *Pause.*

We keep silent and we start to feel uneasy.

BEATRICE   Uneasy about what?

JOHN   Uneasy about being locked in here together. We're suffocating. We need to escape. We're scared—

BEATRICE   Scared?

JOHN   Scared that something is about to happen. Something terrible.

BEATRICE   What could happen?

JOHN   We keep silent.

>   *Pause.*

BEATRICE   Right. We keep silent and let a little time go by. Love grows stronger as time passes.

>   *A long pause. They look at one another.*

Each passing second is like a year. A year of our life together.

She counts, very softly, to ten.

Happy anniversary, darling. Ten years! It's unbelievable how
quickly the time has passed. Did you buy me a present? What
is it? You shouldn't have. We're good together, don't you
think so? Why don't you say something? You never say
anything. It gets on my nerves. Sorry, I don't mean that.
I bought you something too. Look. You like it? We're good
together, don't you think so? Nothing to say?

JOHN says nothing.

Okay. We let a little more time pass. Ten years is not enough.

She counts.

Twenty-five, twenty-six, twenty-seven, twenty-eight, twenty-
nine, thirty. We've been together here for thirty years. You've
put on weight, so have I. You've got back problems, I suffer
from arthritis. We don't talk much. We drink our morning
coffee together. We think about what lies ahead: the body
decays, life shrinks, death. We tell ourselves it doesn't matter
if we get on one another's nerves, as long as there's a hand to
squeeze when the inevitable moment arrives. We think about
the fights we've had, right here in this room, and it makes us
smile. My search for something enchanting, exultant, which
would transform me completely. Your stubbornness, your
reluctance, your obsession with solitude and freedom, my
lies, your violence, our exaggerations, my need to shake you
up so you'll finally say something, your need to hit me so I'll
finally keep silent, it all seems so strange. We search inside
ourselves for the traces of that fire, asking where it came
from. Our bellies? Our brains? It's like a film we haven't seen
for years and years. We can recall certain scenes—terrible
anger, body pushed passionately against body—but we can't
remember what drove the characters. Why did she lock him
in? Why did he want to hit her? We've forgotten. We drink
our coffee without a word, you put your hand on mine, like
you do every morning, before starting the day. As a reminder
that the hand will be there, later, when it's really important.

She takes JOHN's hand and places it on hers.
They stay like that for quite a while.

It hasn't been easy, but it's good that we stayed together, don't you think so? We've become used to each other. We grew old together and eventually we loved one another.

Pause.

JOHN Beatrice…

BEATRICE I… I need to tell you…

JOHN What?

BEATRICE My name is not Beatrice.

JOHN What is it? Diane, Monique, Sylvia, Janet, Martha, Carol? Listen to me, Diane, Monique, Sylvia, Janet—

BEATRICE I'm not Diane or Monique or—

JOHN Listen. If I stay here, I'll die.

BEATRICE Why?

JOHN I'll die from all the rewards I should have received but never did. I'll die drowned in your words, your ideas, your lies. I'll suffocate. I'll die buried alive on the thirty-third floor of an abandoned building.

BEATRICE But you're going to die anyway, in the street, in the shower, in a bar, on a mountaintop while raising a flag, or at the bottom of a river scrounging through wreckage in search of a reward which may not even exist. You might as well die with me, here, quietly.

They remain as they are. She takes his hand.

JOHN I don't want to die quietly. I want to get out of here.

BEATRICE But we're locked in.

JOHN I know.

Pause.

BEATRICE I could be drowning. Right here in this room. Stretched out on the floor, swimming, I could run out of air and shout for help and you could save me.

JOHN Don't, Beatrice.

BEATRICE   You could save me.

JOHN   Stop.

BEATRICE   And we could feel our breath mingle and—

JOHN   And time would pass and I wouldn't recognize you anymore, and I'd resent you for that, but you wouldn't understand and you would drive me crazy trying to get inside me, and I would resist, and one fine day I'd pick up a knife.

BEATRICE   A knife?

JOHN   A knife. Maybe in the middle of a fight, while we're screaming at each other, accusing each other of the same old things, I pick up a knife and point it at you.

BEATRICE   And what do I do?

JOHN   You're too surprised to say anything. You stand there. Terrified.

> *BEATRICE doesn't say anything.*

I come close to you, my hands are shaking, and you run away from me and try to save yourself, but the door is locked and the key is gone and so you start screaming.

BEATRICE   What do I scream?

JOHN   You scream, "Help! Help me! He's locked me in! Help!"

BEATRICE   And does anybody come?

JOHN   No. Nobody comes. Nobody hears you, but you go on screaming, you beat on the walls with your fists and your feet.

BEATRICE   And what do you do?

JOHN   I watch you beating. I'm hot and out of breath as if I'd been running for miles or as if I'd had to climb up thirty-three floors on foot.

BEATRICE   Do you say anything?

JOHN I mutter something like, "You have no right, you can't..."

BEATRICE "You can't" what?

JOHN You can't take what belongs to me.

BEATRICE And what do I answer?

JOHN You don't answer. You continue to beat on the walls with all your might. And I come closer.

BEATRICE And I fall to my knees.

JOHN And I see you on your knees in front of me, and my left hand wants to touch your hair, but my right hand is raised to strike.

BEATRICE And I beg you. I say, "I beg you," just like in a play.

JOHN But I don't hear a word. There's a buzzing inside my head.

BEATRICE I beg you, John.

JOHN I see you lift your hands, and I see your lips move, but I don't hear a word.

BEATRICE I beg you, love me.

JOHN There's a screaming inside my head. It screams, "Do it! Do it, once and for all. She has no right. She can't. She has no right to take what belongs to you."

BEATRICE I beg you, save me.

JOHN There's a howling inside my head. There's an unbearable shrill whistling, and my hands are shaking and—

BEATRICE And I'm screaming "No! No! No! Don't do it!" And, at the last moment, you stop, you take me in your arms, and we—

JOHN You scream, "No! No!" And all of a sudden my right arm rises up so high—

BEATRICE It rises but you stop it.

JOHN   My arm rises and then strikes down hard into your breast.

BEATRICE   No!

JOHN   My arm rises again and strikes a second time and I scream, "Leave me! Leave me alone!"

BEATRICE   Stop, John.

JOHN   I see your lips move but I don't hear the words, and my nose is running, my eyes are running and my red hand grips the knife like a steel vice and my arm strikes, strikes, strikes, and I say, "You don't understand, I can't—"

BEATRICE   Stop now.

JOHN   "I can't, I don't want to give you what you want," and my arm strikes through your breast—

> *Pause.*

BEATRICE   John.

JOHN   And then you keep silent and your body stops moving.

> *A long pause.*

I stay there a long time, crouched down beside you. I look at your opened breast. With my left hand I gently touch your hair. I am exhausted, as if I'd been battling a hurricane. I whisper, "What you wanted from me just scared me to death, can't you understand?"

> *Pause.*

BEATRICE   No. That's not true.

JOHN   Afterwards. Long afterwards, I hear something. Somebody knocking at the door. I don't move. A voice shouts, "Is anybody there?" I don't answer. They knock again. Louder. There are footsteps in the hallway, excited – a lot of them, buzzing. Then, all of a sudden, there's this awful noise. They batter the door down. They come in. They see me. They see you. They back up. Somebody gasps.

BEATRICE   No. You're wrong.

JOHN   Somebody gasps and asks me, "Why?" I say, "She wanted to open me up with a chainsaw, she wanted to cut me in half, she wanted to put her hand into my chest and take what belongs to me. It was self-defense."

A long pause.

BEATRICE   No. It doesn't happen like that.

JOHN   Yes, it happens like that, because of your craziness, and my fear of being locked in, my fear of running out of air—

BEATRICE   No. Listen. We fight, that's true, and you raise your arm to me, but I hang onto you with all my strength, and all of a sudden you fall to your knees and ask me to forgive you and I touch your hair and I say, "Stand up," and we're both shaking with emotion, and we try to understand what is happening to us, and we talk about this need to kill one another which sometimes sweeps over us like a tidal wave, and you take me in your arms and—

JOHN   No, Beatrice.

BEATRICE   You take me in your arms and we say to one another that we have cheated death. And that this is surely what it means to love.

JOHN   No, Beatrice.

Pause.

BEATRICE   Take me in your arms. Please.

She moves close to JOHN. He takes her delicately in his arms.

Save me, John.

JOHN   I can't.

BEATRICE   I beg you. Save me.

JOHN   I can't save you, Beatrice.

With his left hand, he touches BEATRICE's hair. With his right hand, he takes out the knife.

> *She looks at him. She backs away. He walks across the room.*
>
> *After a moment, he drives the knife into the wall beside the door. It opens a hole in the wall, which is made of mere canvas or paper. Through this new opening, a harsh light pours into the room.*

BEATRICE   What did you—? What are you doing?

JOHN   I'm leaving, Beatrice.

> *BEATRICE touches her cheek. She realizes that her face is wet with tears.*

BEATRICE   I'm crying. Look, John, I'm crying!

> *JOHN goes out through the opening he has made in the wall.*

Wait! I'm crying! I'm crying, I'm crying.

> *Through her tears, she smiles at the sheer pleasure of crying.*

I'm crying. I'm crying.

> *After a moment, there is a knock at the door. She moves to the new opening in the wall and tries to see who is outside the door.*
>
> *She speaks in a frail, unconfident voice, wet with tears.*

Who's there?

> *Darkness.*

HELEN'S NECKLACE

Helen's Necklace was first produced in English at the Tarragon Theatre Extra Space from October 7 to November 16, 2003 with the following company:

HELEN   Susan Coyne

NABIL and others   Sanjay Talwar

Direction   Edna Holmes
Set and Costume Design   John Thompson
Lighting Design   Andrea Lundy
Sound Design   Matt Swan
Stage Management   Kate Macdonnell
Script Coordinator   Andrea Romaldi

•Characters•

HELEN

NABIL

THE FOREMAN

THE WOMAN

THE MAN

THE VAGRANT

> *A street corner at a busy intersection. In a city of chaos and heat. Constant sounds of traffic, aggressive honking.*

NABIL   Taxi, please?

HELEN   Excuse me. You didn't happen to see…

NABIL   Taxi, please?

HELEN   A small pearl necklace. I think it fell off, around here somewhere.

NABIL   Somewhere, please?

HELEN   It's not like most pearl necklaces. I mean, the pearls aren't strung neatly in a row – they're placed here and there, on invisible threads. Understand?

> *Pause. NABIL says nothing.*

In fact, there are several rows of invisible threads, but they don't hang neatly on top of one another – the pearls just seem to pop up, out of nowhere. It's hard to explain. Each pearl is held by a microscopic knot, but because the threads are invisible, it seems like the pearls are just hanging there, suspended. Understand? As if they were floating around my throat. You didn't see it, did you? My necklace?

> *NABIL says nothing.*

A little while ago, I stopped here, on this very street corner. And you were there, just where you are now. You asked if I wanted a taxi.

NABIL   Taxi, please?

HELEN   I waited quite a while, before crossing the street. I remember I was wiping my throat. It's so hot, I took out my handkerchief to wipe my throat, like this, and I'm sure it must have been then that I…

> *Pause. NABIL says nothing.*

But, of course, it might have happened earlier. I wear it all the time, even at night. It's not the kind of necklace you would normally wear to bed. Not like a gold or silver chain. No, but to me it's... it's so lightweight, I don't even know it's there. It could have fallen off at any point. A moment ago, I was walking past a shop window, and when I glanced at myself, I saw that it was gone. I shouted: "My necklace!" You didn't happen to pick it up? You didn't happen to see somebody pick it up? Please.

NABIL   Taxi, please.... Yes?

       Pause.

HELEN   No.... Wait.... Yes. Yes, okay. A taxi.

NABIL   Where to, please?

HELEN   That way. Straight ahead.

NABIL   *Yalla, yalla!*

HELEN   I get into his taxi. An antique Mercedes, bright red, except for the back doors, one of which is yellow and the other one, olive drab.... We roar off in a cloud of dust. I shout at him: "Careful!" A huge truck nearly cuts us in half. I shout: "That guy must be crazy!" I shout: "The windows! Please! Can you shut the windows?" He shouts back: "Yes, please, lady?" So I act it out for him. Finally he understands. He rolls up the windows.

       Traffic noise subsides.

Off we go. I can see the sea, between the buildings, the posters, the other cars, the electrical lines. The sea. Sometimes I glance up the street ahead of us. I shout: "Careful!" and he laughs. I close my eyes. I review all the places I've been to since I got here. Lots of places. But I can't remember what order they came in. I'm already forgetting. I walked so far. I think about my necklace. That cloud of white around my neck. So fragile. Everybody comments on it. Even that man I stopped on the street to ask for directions. He gave me a big smile. He said: "Your necklace is so lovely, Madame."

NABIL   Where to, please?

HELEN   Into the city. Straight ahead.

NABIL   East? West?

HELEN   To the centre. That way.

NABIL   *Yalla!*

HELEN   I look at the sea. The bluest blue sea, I dreamed about it before I ever came here, when I was thousands of miles away, at home. I touch my throat. I want to cry. But I don't. We move into the city centre, a huge intersection, and then everything stops. I look up ahead, to see what's going on. Traffic jam.

> *He turns on the radio. Pulsating Arab music is heard.*

He moves his head to the beat of the song. Then his shoulders and his arms. I close my eyes. I try to remember how many days I've been in this city. Eight? Nine? I can't recall exactly. What day is today? Monday or Tuesday? I think it's Monday. I try to remember when I last noticed my necklace. When did I last know for sure that it was floating around my neck? That man I asked for directions. He reached out and touched the pearls with his fingertips. And where exactly was that? Which neighbourhood? I can't recall. What day was that? Saturday? Friday? We're still stuck in the traffic jam. Cars and trucks as far as you can see. It's so hot. But if I roll down the window, I'll go deaf from all the honking!

> *Pause, during which there's only the sound of the music on the radio.*

How many songs have we listened to, stuck in this traffic jam? Four, five, six, ten? Or just one song, over and over and over again – that's how it seems. *(pause)* "This necklace is lighter-than-air." That's what the guy said, when he sold it to me. I laughed. To describe a necklace like that: lighter-than-air. Oh! What's happening now? We're moving!

> *Radio music grows louder.*

NABIL   Where to, please?

HELEN   The centre.

NABIL   This is the centre.

HELEN   Yes, I know. I'm looking for a construction site. Steel girders and concrete floors. The skeleton of a building. With a crane. You know, a "crane"? A big machine with a long neck and—

NABIL   Where to?

HELEN   And jack-hammers and…. *(suddenly irritable)* Please, turn off the music.

NABIL   Please?

HELEN   The music. Turn it off, please! The music, the music!

> *She gestures to the radio. He understands and turns it off.*

Thank you. A construction site, understand? Where they're building something. A work site. Wait – I think that's it, right over there. *(She points.)* Over there. To the left. *Aa chmèèl.* Careful! Please don't do that. Don't change lanes without signalling. You'll get us both killed. Don't you have blinkers?

NABIL   What, please?

HELEN   Blinkers – turn signals! Never mind. That way. That big street, on your right. *Aal yamine.* Careful. There, straight ahead. That's it! I think that's it. But it's already changed. They've added another floor. Stop. Stop! Please, stop!

NABIL   Stop here?

HELEN   Yes, right here. Wait for me. Understand? Wait right here!

NABIL   Here, yes?

HELEN   Yes. Here, please.

> *Noise of jack-hammers and other construction equipment grows louder. HELEN approaches the FOREMAN of the construction site. His back is to her. She taps him on the shoulder, and shouts:*

Pardon me. Excuse me. Please – you didn't happen to see a little necklace?

THE FOREMAN   What?

HELEN   Did you see a little necklace? Tiny white pearls on invisible threads. Not the sort of pearl necklace you'd ever expect. I mean, the pearls just pop up, almost at random, along the little threads and—

THE FOREMAN   What?

HELEN   I stopped here yesterday. I think it was yesterday. Nobody was around. No workers. I walked all around, and then I sat down, right over there, in the middle. It was so hot, I took out my handkerchief to wipe my face and throat, and that may have been when—

THE FOREMAN   Look around, please, look all around. What do you see?

HELEN   I was right over there, in the middle, I sat there for quite a while, and tried to imagine—

THE FOREMAN   What you see is concrete floors and steel girders, and hard-working men in their boots, and cement which flows through big pipes, and jack-hammers tearing into the sidewalk. This is a work site.

HELEN   Yes, I know, but—

THE FOREMAN   Come on. Come with me.

> *He leads her away from the jack-hammers, and the noise fades considerably.*

HELEN   I was sitting right over there, in the middle, on that concrete floor, for quite a while. I tried to imagine what used to be here. A quaint old stone house with trees all around and flowers in flower-boxes, and people living inside.

THE FOREMAN   Listen to me. For most of my life I've been breaking things down and building things up, right here, in the centre. And always I see people like you, people who come to look for something they lost. A box full of money, a photograph, a little statue of something, an old book, a necklace. They come here and they look at the bulldozers and they walk around the big hole, they scratch in the dirt, and sometimes they come back again later, after we've poured all the concrete, and they walk around on the floor, and they look around everywhere—

HELEN   No, no – you don't understand. I was never here until yesterday, or maybe the day before yesterday, and—

THE FOREMAN   They come here and they cry about the past, about everything they have lost, but I say to them: "Go away! What you have lost is broken in pieces, reduced to dust, and the dust is mixed back into the earth, or into the concrete. Those old things of yours are part of this new building now. And it's much better that way."

HELEN   You don't understand. I never lived here—

THE FOREMAN   I understand, you never lived here, you were not born here, but your aunt, or your grandmother that you never even met, used to live here, and she had this precious necklace, so you have come here, on a pilgrimage, to reclaim her lost treasure. I've got this story memorized.

HELEN   No, you're wrong—

THE FOREMAN   I know how it feels to lose everything. One night they dropped a bomb on my house. We were in the bomb shelter. When we got back, there was nothing left, not one wall standing. I said to my children: "Look at it: that's what a house is, a few bricks, some wood, some concrete. Everything you own can be broken, just like that, reduced to dust." They wanted to dig around in the rubble, to look for their toys, but I said: "No, we will scrape it all away, and then we will build it up again."

HELEN   Please listen. I didn't explain myself very well. I never lived here, neither did my aunt or my grandmother. Nobody ever dropped a bomb on my house. I was never here before yesterday or the day before. I only want to know if, maybe, when you first got here this morning, you happened to see on the floor over there... I know it's not very likely that you would have noticed, but I thought it's worth asking.

THE FOREMAN   So, you want a necklace? Go this way and turn right at the first street, you'll find my cousin Youssef and his little shop. He's got gold chains, silver chains, anything you want. Best jewellery in the city.

HELEN   I don't want the best jewellery in the city, I want my necklace with the little plastic pearls popping up on their invisible threads—

THE FOREMAN   Plastic!

HELEN   A lighter-than-air necklace. That's what he said when he sold it to me. I know it's a ridiculous expression, but—

THE FOREMAN   You are so worried about a plastic necklace!

HELEN   At first I said to him: "No, thanks, I won't even try it on, it's much too expensive." But he insisted. He stood behind me and draped it around my throat. He said: "Go ahead, take a look. It's you. This necklace is you."

THE FOREMAN   So, why did you come here?

HELEN   I told you, I came to look for my—

THE FOREMAN   No. I mean, here, to this country?

HELEN   Because... I—

THE FOREMAN   I will tell you why. You came here to cry about the past, lady – to cry about all that we have broken and all that we have built up again.

HELEN   That's not true. Why would you say that?

THE FOREMAN   It's no use. Go home.

> *He moves back toward the construction site.*
> *Noise of jack-hammers increases again.*

HELEN   (*shouting*) It's not true. I didn't come here for that! I came here for—

THE FOREMAN   (*shouting*) Go home, to your house which has never had a bomb dropped on it, to your country which still has all its pieces.

HELEN   (*shouting*) But I only want—

THE FOREMAN   *(shouting)* Let me get on with my work.
  Go home!

> HELEN *hesitates for a moment, surrounded by the*
> *noise of jack-hammers, then she goes back to the taxi.*

NABIL   Where to, please?

HELEN   *(to NABIL)* He told me, "Go back to your country
  which has all its pieces." But I… I am missing a piece. I am
  missing my necklace with little white pearls on invisible
  threads. I'm missing that white cloud around my neck, and
  I'm missing… so many things.

NABIL   Where to?

HELEN   I don't know.

NABIL   East? West? Where to?

HELEN   He looks at me. He smiles. I nod my head. I don't say
  anything. He turns back around. He waits. He's in no hurry.
  So we wait there on that crooked little street, so narrow that
  the cars have to slow down and climb up onto the sidewalk,
  to get around us. They honk at us and shout insults as they
  squeak past. But he doesn't give a damn. And I don't either.
  "Where to, please?" I don't know. "You came here to cry."
  People move past us on the sidewalk, in a hurry. Going to the
  office, to the grocery store, to the jewellery shop. Across the
  street, an old man is staring at me intensely from his
  newspaper stand. I look away. "You came here to cry, lady."
  But I see myself, smiling, when we finally landed here. How
  long ago is that? Twelve days? Two weeks? I don't recall.
  I remember, the minute we arrived, René stuck his nose
  outside and declared, "The weather's much too nice here for
  us to reflect on the troubles of the world. These conferences
  should only be held in places with a shitty climate."
  Everybody laughed.… That old man is still staring at me.
  I can't meet his look. I feel myself blushing.… The jeweller
  fastened the necklace around my neck. I paid and walked
  out. Beautiful weather. I walked around for hours. I felt
  invincible. Wearing beauty like a shield.… He's still staring at
  me from behind his newspapers. I roll down the window and

I shout at him, "What do you want? What's wrong? Are you hoping that I will cry? You think I came here to cry?"

NABIL   Yes… please… lady?

HELEN   Let's go. *Yalla!*

NABIL   Where to?

HELEN   I don't…. That way.

NABIL   *Yalla!*

HELEN   We cruise down the little streets. I tell him, "This way – that way. *Aa chmèèl, aal yamine,*" but I have no idea where I'm going. Sometimes I recognize a building, or a street corner, or a terrace. I was there, once. I had a cup of coffee on that terrace. When? I can't recall exactly. I tell him, "*Aa chmèèl, aal yamine,*" and he follows my directions without hesitation. We get into a neighbourhood where all the houses have gaping holes where walls used to be. I've been here before, I'm certain. I try to get my bearings. We weave through streets crowded with people, a fruit and vegetable market, everything ripe and gleaming, huge photographs of men in turbans. I shout at him: "Stop. Here, please."

NABIL   Here, please?

HELEN   Wait for me…. I step out onto the street. Two boys are running down the sidewalk and nearly knock me down. I shout at them: "Careful!" One of them turns around, smiles at me, then laughs and disappears around the corner. I walk past the gaping holes where walls used to be, past men with great moustaches and women invisible behind their white robes. I was here before. I'm certain. I bought an orange over there – in that improvised grocery store, the dark door into the building which is mostly gone now. I ate an orange while walking down this street, I'm almost sure. And I stopped in front of that building there, to look at the flowers which are growing up through the shattered concrete. Then I went even closer, and I put my fingers into the bullet holes. Why would I do such a thing? I have no idea – because I couldn't stop myself. And then, I went down a narrow little passageway. Where was it? Right here, I think it was. I creep along between rows of houses, where there's a bit of shade. I was definitely here before. I look down. If my necklace fell off here, then it's been trampled by hundreds, thousands of feet. Dozens of people could've seen it, picked it up, sold it, given it to someone else, thrown it in the garbage, or kept it for themselves. I know. But I scour the ground with my eyes all the same, I peer into all the little cracks at the foot of the wall. I pass beneath a crumbling arch and find myself in an even narrower alley, which I also recognize, I'm almost sure of it, I stopped here before, I leaned against that wall, right over there, beside that window. I make my way toward it. And then a woman steps up to me. Where did she come from? Without a sound, she is just suddenly there.

A WOMAN has appeared.

HELEN   *(to her)* Excuse me, you didn't happen to see—?

THE WOMAN   *(interrupting) La twakhizni indak tabé hamra?*

HELEN   Sorry – I don't understand.

THE WOMAN   Did you happen to see a red rubber ball?

HELEN   No…. No, I don't think so. But did you happen to see a necklace? I was here before, I think, and it may have slipped off. A necklace of tiny white pearls—

THE WOMAN   The ball belongs to my son. A small red rubber ball, almost new. No bigger than this. It may have rolled down this alley. Did you happen to see?

HELEN   No. It's not here. See? If it were here, we'd notice it right away. We'd see a ball, especially a red one, but my necklace – it's so fragile. Lighter-than-air. That's what he said when he sold it to me.

THE WOMAN   Lighter-than…?

HELEN   It means… I think he meant that it's so delicate, so flimsy, it could easily get lost. I know it's silly: "lighter-than-air," it doesn't make sense, but when he said that to me, I suddenly felt—

THE WOMAN   Will you go with me, and look?

HELEN   For the ball which belongs to your son?

THE WOMAN   And for the necklace, if you like.

HELEN   I'm not really sure—

THE WOMAN   Come on.

HELEN   She leads me. Down the narrow alley. She opens a door, into a courtyard. We go in. We search through the dusty grass with our feet. I was never in this courtyard before. We come out the other side, into a much wider street. Two men at a sidewalk café are sharing the *narghile* – a water-pipe. The woman asks them something, probably "You didn't happen to see a small red rubber ball and a necklace of tiny white pearls?" One of the men speaks to her. She interrupts him, gesturing excitedly. She says to me: "*Yalla! Yalla!*" And we plunge back into the narrow streets, among broken houses. We turn *aa chmèèl, aal yamine, aa chmèèl, aal yamine*. She seems to know exactly where she's going, following a map in her mind. Sometimes we stop to look under a big stone, or into an old garbage can, we push scraps of rusty iron aside with our feet. We pass through the neighbourhood faster and faster. A woman shouts something at us from her third-story window. I think I recognize the name "Sarah." Is my fellow searcher called Sarah? She shouts back and gestures excitedly, as if to say "Let me get on with this!" And now we move even faster, until our way is blocked by a house that is more missing than present. We walk into this house through a huge wound in the wall. She says to me, "Come on." We squeeze through another hole in another wall, and arrive at a staircase. We climb up as fast as we can. On the second floor, we hear voices coming from behind tall green curtains. It sounds like a mother and her son, arguing, shouting. We continue up the staircase – third floor – fourth floor. The staircase gets narrower and narrower, till it stops before a small door. The woman opens it, takes my arm and pulls me outside. We are on the roof. I'm suddenly dizzy. I teeter toward the edge.

THE WOMAN   Help me look.

HELEN   But there's no point. I was never here before.

THE WOMAN   Look down there. Look all around.

HELEN   We're too high up. I could never see it from way up here.

THE WOMAN   Everybody says this: "A little rubber ball, you could never see it from so far away." But I say to myself, "How can they be sure?" Help me look.

> *Pause. They both search the neighbourhood which spreads out below them.*

HELEN   When did your son lose the rubber ball? I'm asking because I don't really know exactly when my necklace slipped off. So I don't really know where I ought to look for it.

THE WOMAN   He left the house at about ten o'clock with his friend Wallid. He ran past me, and I shouted, "Are you not forgetting something?" He turned round and said, "That's right, my red rubber ball." I said, "You forgot to give your old mother a kiss, my son." He blushed. He gave me a kiss on the cheek and then he ran out.

HELEN   And now everybody teases him, "What's so important about a red rubber ball? Just buy another one!" But he wants to find that one. Maybe he always felt invincible, bouncing the red rubber ball. I know, from the moment I bought my necklace, I wore it everywhere, always, and it helped me to feel so much more confident.

THE WOMAN   Look, down there! Do you see a little spot of red?

HELEN   Where exactly?

THE WOMAN   There – there – at the edge of the street.

HELEN   Well… no… I can't see it. Has he been out all day, looking for it – your son?

> *Pause.*

THE WOMAN   They came to my house around eleven o'clock. I heard them shouting from the stairs, "Sarah! Sarah!" I was shelling beans in the kitchen. I always cook beans on

Monday. All of a sudden, I felt so warm. I lost my balance – had to lean against the table. They sang out, "Sarah! Sarah!" like birds at daybreak. I opened the door. Amir said to me, "Your son, Sarah. Your son." They brought me to this street, right down there. They showed me the body of a young boy covered with blood, with his face blown away. Everything changed from red to black. I fell down. When I came to, they were splashing water in my face, and everybody was talking to me at once. "This is dreadful. You must be strong. He was caught in the crossfire. Your son was in the wrong place at the wrong time. We do not know who shot him. This neighbourhood has been safe for weeks now. The war is almost over. It says so in the newspaper." I pushed them all away, and told them, "That is not my son." "Yes, Sarah, it is your son." "No! That poor boy has no face. My son has a face." "But aren't these his clothes? Look at him – it is your son." "No, it's not him. My son has a smile which lights up the room, and a little scar on his right cheek, where he fell down the stairs when he was three and a half. My son was with his friend Wallid. My son had a little red rubber ball in his hand. So where is the rubber ball? Tell me that!"

Pause.

HELEN   I'm so sorry. I didn't know. I didn't understand.

THE WOMAN   I buried that boy whose face was gone and everyone said how sorry they were. They sobbed and shook my hand. As soon as they left me alone, I started to search.

HELEN   So, it's been a long time since… since your son lost the rubber ball.

THE WOMAN   Yes, a long long time.

HELEN   But you're still searching.

THE WOMAN   Not every day. Only on Mondays. I search all the streets in the neighbourhood, and then I climb up here, so I can see everything in one glance.

HELEN   And you still think he's—

THE WOMAN   I don't think anything. I come here and
I search. Mostly I do not discover anything important, but
sometimes I suddenly see – Look, over there!

HELEN   Where?

THE WOMAN   Right there. Quite far away, at the edge of the
neighbourhood, where the highway cuts across. Look very
hard. Do you see a little spot of red, bouncing up and down.
Look. It's getting closer. It's coming this way. It's a rubber
ball, I can see it clearly now, a red rubber ball somebody is
tossing up and then catching in his hand. Do you see the
hand? Connected to the hand there is an arm, and connected
to the arm there is a body. The body of a young man.
Seventeen years old. He's coming this way. We have to wave
to him. *(She waves excitedly.)* Go ahead, you must wave too.

> *HELEN hesitates, but then waves shyly in the same
> direction.*

And now, we must call to him. Call with me: Mounir!
Mounir!

> *HELEN hesitates, but then joins in the calling:*

HELEN   Mounir! Mounir!

THE WOMAN   Mounir! Mounir! *(suddenly anxious, to HELEN)*
Do you think he will recognize me? My face is so wrinkled
now, and my eyes have changed. Everything about me has
changed. My look, and my skin, and my heart... Mounir!
What is he doing? He is going away. Mounir! Where has he
gone? Did you see?

HELEN   Please, I don't—

THE WOMAN   I cannot see him anymore. *(pause.)* You see, it is
always at this moment that I start to cry. Look. They just
come pouring out. I cannot stop them. Cry with me, if you
want to, cry for my son – who is lighter-than-air.

HELEN   I didn't know...

THE WOMAN   Or cry for your lost necklace. Look down at
this neighbourhood, and beyond, at this whole city, and say

to yourself, "I will never find it again. Never!" *Abadan! Abadan!*

> *Both women look out at the city. From a nearby mosque, a muezzin calls the faithful to prayer through a loud-speaker.*

HELEN   She cries out, *"Abadan, abadan, abadan"* for a long time. I think about her son, and his red rubber ball, and his faceless face, and about a young man who smiled at me in the street the first day I wore my necklace and suddenly the world belonged to me, about my country which still has all its pieces, about all those pieces of the puzzle which I lack: confidence, beauty, passion, love, and what else? About Sarah who's afraid her own son won't recognize her, about her wrinkled face, about her searching eyes, about all those little white pearls rattling around somewhere in this city, and I hear Sarah crying beside me, and the loud-speakers crying out words I can't understand, probably "Come, one and all, and cry that Allah alone is great," but I imagine they are crying, "Come, one and all, and cry for the son of Sarah, and for Helen's necklace, cry for their faces which are no longer the same, for their joy which has vanished."

THE WOMAN   That is good for now. Time to go home.

HELEN   She leads me back downstairs. On the second floor, the mother and her son have stopped shouting at each other. The mother opens the tall green curtains and comes up to Sarah. I can see her son sitting in the background, a boy of about sixteen or seventeen. His mother speaks to him, and I think I hear the word "Wallid." Wallid? She touches Sarah's face so gently, and says something to her. Perhaps "Yes, your son is dead, Sarah. You have to accept it." Or maybe she says, "Did you see him today? Did you speak to him?" Sarah says nothing. We go back to the street.

THE WOMAN   This is my way. Goodbye.

> *THE WOMAN starts out.*

HELEN   Wait. I want to tell you—

THE WOMAN   To tell me? That you are sorry for me? This is not necessary. You are not really sorry.

HELEN   But I—

THE WOMAN   But it doesn't matter. I am not sorry about your necklace. Goodbye.

HELEN   She goes away. Walking very fast, she turns the corner and disappears. I slump down on the ground. Leaning against the wall of a shattered house. Where am I now? What street, what city, what country? I don't recall. What am I doing here? "You came here to cry, lady." I stay there. For a long time. An old woman walks past, then a little girl, chasing her cat. As if I weren't there.

NABIL   Please? Lady?

HELEN   What are you—

NABIL   Please, lady.

HELEN   What are you doing here? How did you find me?

NABIL   Taxi, please. Taxi.

HELEN   He takes my hand and helps me up. His hand is so warm, as I hold it. So comforting. As if he gathered all of me up in his one warm hand. I let him lead me. I squeeze his hand, to say "Thank you. Thank you for having such a warm hand, and thank you for knowing the way." He stops and gestures for me to wait. In a moment, he's back with two cups of coffee. He gestures for me to taste it. I choose the sweeter one. We drink. It's so good, the coffee running down my throat. Like a warm interior caress. He smiles.... What is your name?

NABIL   Please? What?

HELEN   Your name? My name is Helen.

NABIL   Ellen?

HELEN   No, Helen, like the woman who caused the war. You understand?

NABIL   The war?

HELEN   Some people say she was just a plaything of the gods, that it wasn't really her fault, but others say she was guilty, and that she was just as responsible for what happened as if she had wanted it to happen. Helen of Troy. You understand?

NABIL   You are "Helen of Troy," yes?

HELEN   No. Just Helen. Helen of the North. Helen who didn't cause a war. Helen who doesn't know anything about war. And you are?... Mounir? Wallid? Youssef?

NABIL   Nabil.

HELEN   Nabil. Excellent. Hello, Nabil.

> *She shakes his hand. He smiles.*

NABIL   Hello. *Marhaba…*

HELEN   Have you ever lost anything, Nabil?

NABIL   *Marhaba, tcharaffna.*

HELEN   Ever lost a ring, or a watch which you loved very much? And then you felt like an amputee. As if you lost your finger along with the ring, or your arm along with the watch.

NABIL   Taxi, please?

HELEN   Yes, Nabil. Taxi.

NABIL   *Yalla!*

HELEN   We weave through the narrow streets, and all of a sudden we are back at the red Mercedes. Is this where I asked him to wait? I thought it was much further away.

NABIL   Where to, Miss Helen?

HELEN   To the sea.

NABIL   Where to?

HELEN   To the sea. Water as far as you can see. *(She gestures.)* The endless blue. The waves. The sea, Nabil.

NABIL   *Oh. El bahr! El bahr!*

HELEN   That's right, *el bahr.* I guess that's right.

NABIL   *El bahr kbiir.* Which way, Miss Helen?

HELEN   That way. *Yalla!*

NABIL   *Yalla!*

HELEN   We depart again. It's so hot. The sun beats down on the Mercedes. Suddenly I think of my colleagues. Home again in their cool Northern country. What must they have thought when they got my note? "Dear Colleagues, You should leave without me. I've decided to stay on for a while in order to…." In order to? What did I write after that? I can't recall. They must have been astounded. "Helen has lost interest in us," René would say, "She's fallen in love with an Arab prince." The others would laugh at that. "Helen is so secretive. She's been lost in thought ever since we got here." "Everybody's lost in thought at these conferences," René would say, "We're paid to be lost in thought." And everybody would laugh again. But that morning at the airport, they must have felt anxious, they tried calling my hotel room, but nobody answered, and their flight was already boarding. So they left. Where are we now? A different neighbourhood. Was I ever here before? I can't recall. "Look all around down there, think about your necklace, and say to yourself, 'I will never find it again. Never. *Abadan.*'" We're driving alongside a wall which encloses a small town. A separate town within the city. Where is the sea? A man on the sidewalk waits for a break in the traffic so he can cross. We pass by. Suddenly my heart is pounding. Oh my God, isn't that—? That's him, isn't it? I'm sure it is. *(to NABIL)* Stop! Stop here!

NABIL   Here, please? Not the sea here.

HELEN   I don't care. Stop! Wait for me here, Nabil. Please.

NABIL   Not here, please.

HELEN   I understand, you can't park here. Go around the block. *(She gestures.)* Go around a block or two, and come back here to pick me up. Understand?

NABIL   Here, please?

HELEN   Exactly. Right here. In ten minutes. Ten. He drives away. But did he understand? I have no idea. I push my way through the crowd, looking for that man – where is he? There, I see him, but he's walking so fast. *(She shouts.)* Please! Wait just a moment. Please!

THE MAN turns around.

THE MAN   Me?

HELEN   Don't you recognize me? We first saw each other not long ago. It must have been around here somewhere. I can't recall. I was lost. I asked you for directions.

THE MAN   I think you are mistaken.

HELEN   No, no, I approached you, and you were so kind, so polite. You looked at me, and you smiled. It made you smile, a woman like me lost in a city like this. We talked for a minute or two. You asked me where I came from, and I told you about my cold Northern country, where the snow comes down in big white flakes. Then you complimented me on my necklace. Remember? I was wearing a fragile necklace of little white pearls, so light and delicate. You said, "Your necklace is lovely." And you touched it with your fingertips. And I... it seemed wonderful and strange to me, your fingers on my throat, and then we looked into one another's eyes and—

THE MAN   And?

HELEN   And... I have lost it since then, my necklace, and I've been wondering if... if maybe it slipped off and fell at your feet, just when you touched.... Or if it could have fallen into one of your boots, and that evening when you took off your boots, maybe you discovered it.

THE MAN   You have lost your necklace?

HELEN   Exactly, and I was wondering if—

THE MAN   Look at me. I have lost my place. My place on earth. Maybe it fell into one of your shoes? I have lost the place where I can stand and say, "This is mine." Did you happen to discover it when you took off your shoes, that place where I can stand? And I have also lost: "Some day,

I will have a house with a garden." and "Some day, I will travel to a cold Northern land where snow falls in big flakes." and "Some day, my children will have real jobs, they will be doctors or teachers or truck drivers, they will have houses with gardens and they will have a place on this earth." And I have lost: "Look all around, my son, my daughter, this is the earth and it belongs to you. Take it up, explore it, transform it. Make of it what you will." Did that, perhaps, slip into one of your shoes, my children's future? And I have also lost the ability to cry out – maybe you found it inside one of your shoes, my ability to cry out, to beat my fist against the wall. Did you happen to find my cry in your purse, in your blouse, in your throat? Open your mouth.

HELEN   I don't want—

THE MAN   Open your mouth.

> *HELEN opens her mouth.*

Go ahead. You cry out. I want to see. Cry out: "We cannot go on living like this. We cannot go on." Shout it.

HELEN   I'm sorry, I must have been mistaken—

THE MAN   *(seizing her by the shoulders)* Shout it! Cry out!

HELEN   *(quietly, hesitantly)* We cannot go on living like this.

THE MAN   Louder, much louder!

HELEN   *(louder, crying out)* We cannot go on living like this. We cannot go on living like this.

THE MAN   *(shaking her)* Louder!

HELEN   *(crying out as loud as she can)* We cannot go on living like this! We cannot go on living like this! Stop! Please, stop!

> *He lets her go. She stops shouting.*
> *Trembling, she looks into his eyes.*

THE MAN   Forgive me. I did not mean to. I do not know what possessed me. Today is one of my dark days. There are days of light when I manage to forget that I have been walled up inside a camp since the day I was born. I look at my children and they look beautiful to me, I get busy, I eat and drink, I make use of the day which God has given us, I live life like you or like anybody else. But then there are days of darkness, when I see only the wall which walls us in, our houses piled on top of one another, the lack of space and privacy, the filth, the ugliness, and I say to myself, over and over for hours, "This is my only life, I will never have another, this is my only life, and I will live it here," and then when I see people like you walking down the street, people from somewhere else who do not give a damn about my despair—

HELEN   We do give a damn. But we can't – we can't seem to do anything. What can we do?

THE MAN   I do not know. Maybe, when you go home to your own country, to that little place which belongs to you, sometimes you should say, "We cannot go on living like this." When you go to a party with your friends, when you are drinking wine, when you look out the window at your white city, so quiet and so organized, say these words, even if no one understands, even if you do not remember yourself where the phrase comes from, because it is from so long ago, from so far away, from the other side of the earth. Say it.

HELEN   We cannot go on living like this.

THE MAN   Promise me.

> *Pause.*

HELEN   I do. I promise you. *(She starts out.)*

THE MAN   Wait. You said you had lost something?

HELEN   No, nothing. It's not important.

THE MAN   Did you say a necklace?

HELEN   Yes, a necklace. But I was mistaken. You're not the man I asked for directions.

THE MAN   No, I was not that man. But you can ask me now, if you wish.

HELEN   It's no longer necessary. Here's my taxi.

THE MAN   Why is a necklace so important? *(smiling)* Is it a gift from your lover?

HELEN   Yes, exactly. The man who gave it to me loved me so much, then he died, a little while later, in my arms. The necklace is all I have left of him.

THE MAN   I am sorry.

HELEN   I get into the red Mercedes. Nabil says, "Where to, please? *El bahr?*" There's a raft of cars behind us, all honking. I say, "Yes, *el bahr*." We set forth. I turn and look at the man on the sidewalk. He waves. I try to fix his face in my memory. A bus stops between him and me. I've lost him. "We cannot go on living like this." I see Robert, all of a sudden, sitting across from me in our living room, twelve years ago, his head hanging, his face in his hands, and I hear my voice, shaking, breaking the long silence: "We don't love each other anymore, Robert, so we cannot go on living like this." The ache, the bitterness distilled in those words. Is it the same? No, absolutely not. I recall the man on the sidewalk. His hands, shaking me. The fury in his eyes. And there I stood, crying out like a child who is being scolded. *(to NABIL)* Nabil? Did you ever tell a lie, to make yourself seem more interesting?

NABIL   Please?

HELEN   Did you ever invent a tragic history for yourself, just because your little private grief suddenly seemed so... indecent?

NABIL   *El bahr* now?

HELEN   Yes, to the sea, Nabil. We arrive at the sea. He wants to stop, but I say, "No, go further, go on, there's too much concrete here, too many cars and electrical lines." We go on beneath the bluest blue sky. I see myself shoving the envelope under René's door, at four o'clock in the morning. "Dear Colleagues, I've decided to stay on for a while in order to...." I see myself hurrying out of the hotel, fast as I can, running through the deserted streets without memorizing a single landmark, watching the sun come up, stopping for a cup of

sweet coffee. I have no idea where I am, my heart is
pounding so fast, I picture my colleagues departing for the
airport in a shiny new taxi, maybe a little anxious about me.
"Are you sure we should just leave her here?" "Listen, Helen
does whatever she likes." "Shouldn't one of us wait for her?"
"I'm telling you, she met somebody. I saw her talking to some
moody Swedish guy. She's got a crush on somebody. What
else could it be?" A silence falls among them. That's right:
what else could it be? We drive along. Wait – what's that,
over there? Beyond the trees, are those pillars? I can't see.
I shout out, *"Aal yamine, aal yamine, Nabil."* He turns. And
there they are again. White pillars, I see four or five or six of
them. My heart is pounding. "That way, Nabil. Down there.
Quickly!" He parks on a little side-road. I say, "Up there, up
there, I want to see those pillars." He doesn't speak. He takes
my hand and pulls me, leads me to a grove of trees, he parts
the branches, and we take a path, hurrying, hurrying along,
and then climbing up a little cliff, and suddenly, up above us,
a tremendous view. Dozens and dozens of pillars, rows of
them, some in perfect condition, some broken, a sort of army
of pillars, marching down to the sea. And also the sunken
remains of a wall, hundreds of white stones, standing there,
perfectly arranged. A perfect blend of symmetry and chaos.
A perfect blend of grandeur and decay.

NABIL   *Hélou.* Beautiful.

HELEN   Yes, it's beautiful, Nabil. We climb down carefully
among the stones. We descend between the regal pillars.
He's still holding my hand. We walk like newlyweds, or like
victims to the sacrificial altar. We don't speak. He helps me
climb up onto a broken column. I sit down. He gestures for
me to wait there, and he goes away. I sit and look all around.
I think of the man who shook me. I try to recall his face with
an artist's precision. But I can't recall the exact shape of his
eyes, the precise angle of his nose. "We cannot go on living
like this." (*She raises her voice.*) We cannot go on living like
this.

THE VAGRANT   Please?

HELEN   (*startled*) Oh! You scared me!

THE VAGRANT   Lady is angry now?

HELEN   No. I'm not angry.

THE VAGRANT   First time here?

HELEN   Yes, I was never here before.

THE VAGRANT   Thousand-year-old civilization. Wonders of the world. If you like, I show you something. *(He takes something from his pocket.)* Look, four hundred years before your Jesus Christ. Found in the sea. Put back together, stone by stone. Princess' necklace. For you, only one hundred dollars. Very cheap, please.

HELEN   A necklace?

THE VAGRANT   Yes, please. Magnificent necklace. I caught it from the sea. Very old. Two thousand four hundred years. For you. Try it, please.

He tries to put the necklace on her.

HELEN   No, please don't bother.

THE VAGRANT   Yes, you try it, lady. *(He puts it around her neck.)* You Princess now. Look. Magnificent. All men will be after you.

HELEN   Really, I don't want—

THE VAGRANT   Eighty dollars. Very cheap. Imagine, please. Here, two thousand four hundred years, Princess walks and necklace falls into the sand, or Princess gets into boat and leans over to look, and necklace falls into the sea.

HELEN   Yes, I understand. The necklace fell but she didn't notice. And everyone said to her, "It's not serious, it's just a necklace, don't make such a fuss." But she went on searching, for hours and hours, in the sand. And then she went to sea and gazed into the depths and out across the waves, hoping to see it rise from the sea, although that was clearly ridiculous. And after a while she said to herself, "I will never find it again. Never." I loved it so much though, my necklace of tiny white pearls, even if they were plastic. The man who sold it to me said—

THE VAGRANT   Plastic? No, please, lady. Precious stones. True stones.

HELEN   "This necklace is you. It's absolutely you." I walked out onto the street. The sun was shining. A young man smiled at me. I felt so alive, lighter-than-air, with a cloud of beauty around my neck. But now I've lost it. It slipped away across my breast, down my belly and my legs, and I didn't feel a thing. And now I can cry for hours, for days, for years. As if I had lost every man who ever smiled at me, and every blissful afternoon when I believed I had a place on earth, and all my assumptions, one assumption for each tiny pearl: that the world will get better, and that we have a thousand years of life, every one of us, in which to love, to change, to accomplish something, and that we are not really alone, that we can cross over the borders which separate me from you, the thin membranes which envelop each of us, inside which we dream and suffer and suffocate, that we can gently penetrate them without tearing them, and that we can truly reach one another and cry for one another and cry out for one another and the cry will sound exactly right, and shatter all the walls which shut us in.

THE VAGRANT   What do you say, please? I cannot understand. Necklace found again. Fished up by me from the sea. You want to buy?

HELEN   No, I don't want to buy.

THE VAGRANT   Why not? You do not see it beautiful?

HELEN   Yes. Yes, I see it beautiful. But it's not real and it's too heavy.

THE VAGRANT   Real, yes, please. True. Two thousand four hundred years—

HELEN   It's heavy and it will make me heavy and I won't feel alive and lighter-than-air when I wear it, but that's not your fault.

She takes off the necklace and returns it to THE VAGRANT.

THE VAGRANT   Fifty dollars only.

HELEN   I said no. Go away now. I don't want the necklace.
Not now.

THE VAGRANT   You want to see other things? Come with me.
Down there. More wonders. Rings. Bracelets. Two thousand
five hundred, two thousand six hundred years. Come on.

HELEN   No. Go away, get away from me!

THE VAGRANT goes away.

He goes away, making gestures which I can't understand.
Now he's far away, but still gesturing. "Come, please.
Wonders of the world." He walks over a sand dune. I don't
see him anymore. I sit on the broken column. A woman of
marble contemplating the sea. "Dear Colleagues, I've decided
to stay on for a while in order to... to lose something. I think
this is a good place to do that. Please don't worry." I walk
down to the water's edge. I make footprints in the wet sand.
On the frothy crest of a wave, all of a sudden I see my
necklace appear for a moment, something ridiculously small
and delicate which boils up for a moment and evaporates just
as quickly. I reach out to grab it. Ridiculous. My arm is much
too short. I close my hand around emptiness, like that. I open
my fist. Nothing.

NABIL appears behind her.

NABIL   Please, lady. *(He holds something out to her.)*

HELEN   Nabil!

NABIL   For you.

HELEN   What is it? A stone?

NABIL   From my country, please.

HELEN   Thank you, Nabil. I will be careful not to lose it.
I promise. I'll hold it so tightly in my hand. Thank you.
(She kisses him on the cheek.) And I'd like to ask you.... Would
you put your arm around my neck? Just for a moment.
Understand? Like a shield. *(She stands in front of him and rests*

her back against his chest. She takes his arm and wraps it around her neck.)

NABIL   We lose things, Helen. You must accept this. But you still have your neck and your hands, one to hold tightly the stone that I gave you, and another for… I don't know—

HELEN   But Nabil – you—?

NABIL   You still have your eyes, your arms, your mouth for eating, speaking, crying, kissing a man like me on the cheek—

HELEN   Nabil, you—

NABIL   You still have so many things.

HELEN   You are speaking—

NABIL   *(He steps away from her.)* Yes, please.

HELEN   You seem able to…. Or is it that I am suddenly able to understand Arabic?

>*Pause.*

NABIL   Taxi, please?

>*Pause.*

HELEN   Yes, taxi, Nabil.

>*He takes her hand and they start out.*

Wait. Right here. Ten seconds. Only ten seconds.

>*She lets go of NABIL's hand and approaches the audience.*

We cannot go on living like this. We cannot go on living like this.

NABIL   Let's go, please.

HELEN   I'm ready now, Nabil. *Yalla!*

photo by Lorne Huston

About the Playwright

Carole Fréchette has been a force in Québec theatre for more than 25 years. Her plays, translated in several languages, are performed all over the world. She won the 1995 Governor General's Award for her play *Les Quatre morts de Marie* (*The Four Lives of Marie*) and the 1998 Chalmers Award for the same play translated into English. She then received Governor General's Award nominations for *La Peau d'Élisa* (*Elisa's Skin*) in 1998, for *Les Sept jours de Simon Labrosse* (*Seven Days in the Life of Simon Labrosse*) in 1999 and for *Jean et Béatrice* (*John and Beatrice*) in 2002. Her play *Le Collier d'Hélène* (*Helen's Necklace*) recently earned her the Sony Labou Tansi Award in France. In 2002, the French association SACD (Société des auteurs et compositeurs dramatiques) awarded her, in Avignon, the Prix de la Francophonie to underline her success in the French-speaking world; the same year, she received in Toronto the Siminovitch Prize, Canada's most prestigious theatre award. Three English translations of her plays by John Murrell, were published under the title *Three Plays* by Playwrights Canada Press in Toronto: *The Four Lives of Marie, Seven Days in the Life of Simon Labrosse* and *Élisa's Skin*. She has also translated Colleen Wagner's *The Monument*.

About the Translator

John Murrell is one of the most frequently produced Canadian playwrights. His plays have been translated into 15 different languages and performed internationally. His work for the stage includes the Canadian classic, *Waiting for the Parade*; *Memoir*, which has been produced world-wide; Chalmers Best Canadian Play Award winners *Farther West* and *The Faraway Nearby*; and the libretto for the acclaimed new opera *Filumena*.

As a translator, he has created frequently revived versions of Chekhov's *Uncle Vanya*, *The Seagull*, and *The Cherry Orchard*; Ibsen's *The Doll House*; Rostand's *Cyrano de Bergerac*; and *The Four Lives of Marie*, *Elisa's Skin*, and *Seven Days in the Life of Simon Labrosse*, all by Carole Fréchette.